TEXT BOOK OF MEDICINAL CHEMISTRY – III (THEORY)

VISHESH KUMAR MAURYA

Made with ❤ on the Notion Press Platform
www.notionpress.com

To those who inspire, support, and uplift.

To my family, whose unwavering belief in my potential has been the bedrock of my journey. Your love, patience, and encouragement have been my greatest sources of strength.

To my friends and mentors, who have guided me with wisdom, shared in my triumphs, and offered solace in times of struggle. Your insights and companionship have made this journey enriching and meaningful.

To the countless researchers and scientists whose dedication to the pursuit of knowledge has laid the groundwork for my endeavors. Your passion and persistence are the torchlights that lead the way.

And to the dreamers and future pioneers, may this work inspire you to explore, innovate, and push the boundaries of what is possible. Your curiosity and determination are the catalysts for a brighter tomorrow.

This work is a testament to the power of collaboration, perseverance, and the human spirit. Thank you for being part of my journey.

Contents

Foreword

In the rapidly evolving landscape of scientific discovery and technological innovation, the field of drug design stands at the forefront of our quest to improve human health. This book, "Advances in Drug Design: From Concept to Cure," is a comprehensive guide that delves into the multifaceted approaches, methodologies, and technologies that are revolutionizing the way we discover and develop new therapeutic agents.

As we navigate the complexities of modern medicine, it is essential to understand the foundations and advancements that drive drug discovery. This book offers a detailed exploration of various strategies, including high-throughput screening, structure-based drug design, ligand-based drug design, and the integration of artificial intelligence and machine learning in predicting drug efficacy and safety. Each chapter provides in-depth knowledge, practical insights, and case studies that illustrate the real-world applications of these approaches.

The importance of multidisciplinary collaboration in drug design cannot be overstated. This book brings together the expertise of chemists, biologists, pharmacologists, and data scientists, showcasing how their collective efforts contribute to the development of new drugs. It emphasizes the critical role of computational tools, such as pharmacophore modeling and molecular docking, in predicting and optimizing drug-target interactions, thereby accelerating the drug discovery process.

The authors have also highlighted the significance of combinatorial chemistry, a technique that has transformed the synthesis of diverse chemical libraries, enabling the rapid identification of potential drug candidates. This book not only covers the theoretical aspects but also provides practical guidance on implementing these techniques in the laboratory.

One of the most compelling features of this book is its forward-looking perspective. It addresses the challenges and future directions in drug design, encouraging readers to think beyond traditional paradigms and consider innovative approaches that could shape the future of medicine. The integration of novel technologies, such as CRISPR for gene editing and personalized medicine, is discussed, offering a glimpse into the potential of these cutting-edge advancements to revolutionize healthcare.

Whether you are a student, researcher, or professional in the field of drug design, this book serves as an invaluable resource. It equips you with the knowledge and tools necessary to understand and contribute to the ever-evolving landscape of drug discovery and development. The comprehensive coverage, combined with practical insights and real-world examples, makes it an essential read for anyone committed to advancing the science of drug design.

As we stand on the brink of new discoveries and innovations, "Advances in Drug Design: From Concept to Cure" is a testament to the ingenuity and dedication of scientists around the world. It is my sincere hope that this book will inspire and empower the next generation of researchers to continue pushing the boundaries of what is possible, ultimately bringing new and effective treatments to those in need.

Preface

The field of medicinal chemistry is at the heart of the pharmaceutical sciences, bridging the gap between the discovery of new chemical entities and their transformation into safe and effective therapeutic agents. This book, "Foundations and Advances in Medicinal Chemistry," is designed to serve as a comprehensive resource for students, researchers, and professionals who are passionate about the art and science of drug design and development.

The journey of this book began with the recognition of a growing need for a text that not only covers the fundamental principles of medicinal chemistry but also addresses the latest advancements and challenges in the field. Our aim has been to create a resource that is both educational and inspirational, providing a thorough grounding in the basics while also exploring cutting-edge technologies and methodologies.

Throughout this book, we have strived to present complex concepts in a clear and accessible manner. The chapters are meticulously structured to build upon each other, starting with foundational topics such as the physicochemical properties of drug molecules, structure-activity relationships (SAR), and the principles of pharmacokinetics and pharmacodynamics. We then delve into more specialized areas, including high-throughput screening, structure-based and ligand-based drug design, and the role of computational tools in modern medicinal chemistry.

A significant portion of this book is dedicated to the discussion of current and emerging technologies that are reshaping the landscape of drug discovery. Topics such as combinatorial chemistry, pharmacophore modeling, molecular docking, and the integration of artificial intelligence and machine learning are explored in depth. By providing detailed explanations and practical examples, we aim to equip readers with the knowledge and skills needed to leverage these tools in their own research.

The real-world application of medicinal chemistry principles is illustrated through numerous case studies and examples. These case studies not only highlight successful drug discoveries but also provide insights into the challenges and setbacks that often accompany the drug development process. Our goal is to provide a realistic perspective on the intricacies of medicinal chemistry, emphasizing the importance of perseverance, innovation, and interdisciplinary collaboration.

One of the unique aspects of this book is its forward-looking approach. In addition to discussing current trends, we have included chapters on future directions in medicinal chemistry, such as personalized medicine, gene therapy, and the development of biologics. We believe that an understanding of these emerging areas is crucial for anyone looking to make a lasting impact in the field.

The creation of this book has been a collaborative effort, and we are deeply grateful to the many contributors who have shared their expertise and insights. Their contributions have enriched the content and ensured that this book reflects the latest advancements and best practices in medicinal chemistry.

In conclusion, "Foundations and Advances in Medicinal Chemistry" is intended to be more than just a textbook. It is a comprehensive guide that we hope will inspire and empower the next generation of medicinal chemists.

Whether you are a student just beginning your journey, a researcher seeking to expand your knowledge, or a professional looking to stay abreast of the latest developments, we trust that you will find this book to be an invaluable resource.

Thank you for joining us on this exciting journey into the world of medicinal chemistry.

Acknowledgements

First and foremost, I would like to thank my family for their unwavering support and encouragement. Your patience, understanding, and belief in me have been my greatest sources of strength throughout this journey. Without your love and support, this book would not have been possible.

I would like to express my profound gratitude to my mentors and colleagues, whose expertise and insights have been invaluable. thank you for your guidance and for always challenging me to think critically and creatively. Your mentorship has been instrumental in shaping my approach to medicinal chemistry.

I am also indebted to the contributors and co-authors who have enriched this book with their knowledge and experience. Your chapters have added depth and breadth to the content, ensuring that this book covers a wide range of topics with the rigor and clarity they deserve.

A special thank you to my research team for your hard work and dedication. Your contributions to the research and the countless hours spent in the lab have been essential in bringing this book to fruition. I am particularly grateful to **Ms. Swati verma , Ms. Maneesha Pathak and Ms. Aaliya Naaz** for your assistance with data collection and analysis.

My sincere thanks to the reviewers and editors who provided valuable feedback and helped refine the manuscript. Your careful scrutiny and constructive suggestions have greatly improved the quality of this book. In particular, I would like to thank **Ms. Aaliya Naaz** for your thorough review and insightful comments.

I am grateful to the publishing team at [Publisher's Name] for your professionalism and support throughout the publishing process. Your expertise in production, marketing, and distribution has been instrumental in bringing this book to a wider audience.

Finally, I would like to thank the students, researchers, and professionals who will read this book. Your pursuit of knowledge and passion for medicinal chemistry are the true inspiration behind this work. It is my hope that this book will serve as a valuable resource in your academic and professional endeavors.

Thank you all for your contributions, support, and encouragement. This book is a testament to the collaborative spirit and shared passion for advancing the field of medicinal chemistry.

Prologue

UNIT – I

Antibiotics

Ehrlich's phase, the empirical period, and the present phase are the three phases that make up the history of chemotherapy. During the early 16th century, Paracelsus employed mercury as a cure for syphilis, and in the 17th century, cinchona bark was utilized to treat pyrexia. Chinese traditional medicine employed molded soybean curd to treat wounds and infections as early as 500–600 BC. During these early periods, leprosy was treated by Hindus using chaulmoogra oil. It was discovered during Ehrlich's phase that some dyes were poisonous and killed some microbes. Ehrlich therefore created neoarsphenamine to treat syphilis. The term "antibiosis" was first used to describe the death of anthrax bacilli in culture media containing other bacteria during the 18th century.

"The term antibiotic has its origin in the word antibiosis (i.e. against life). Antibiotics are chemical substances obtained from various species of microorganisms (bacteria, fungi, actinomycetes) that suppress the growth of other microorganisms and eventually may destroy them. The probable points of difference amongst the antibiotics may be physical, chemical, pharmacological properties, antibacterial spectra, and mechanism of action. They have made it possible to cure diseases caused by bacteria, such as pneumonia, tuberculosis, and meningitis, and they save the lives of millions of people around the world."

Historical Background of Antibiotics:

The history of antibiotics is a testament to human ingenuity in the fight against infectious diseases. It began in earnest in the early 20th century with the groundbreaking work of scientists such as Alexander Fleming, Paul Ehrlich, and Gerhard Domagk.

- **Discovery of Penicillin:** Alexander Fleming's discovery of penicillin in 1928 marked a turning point in medicine. By chance, Fleming noticed that a mold called Penicillium notatum inhibited the growth of bacteria in a petri dish. This accidental discovery laid the foundation for the development of the first antibiotic.
- **Development of Sulfa Drugs:** In the 1930s, German chemist Paul Ehrlich developed the first synthetic antimicrobial agents known as sulfa drugs. These drugs, such as sulfanilamide, were effective against a range of bacterial infections and paved the way for the synthesis of other antibiotics.
- **Mass Production of Antibiotics:** During World War II, the need for effective treatments for wounded soldiers spurred efforts to mass-produce penicillin. This led to the development of techniques for large-scale fermentation and extraction, making antibiotics more widely available.
- **Golden Age of Antibiotics:** The period from the 1940s to the 1960s is often referred to as the "golden age" of antibiotic discovery. During this time, researchers discovered a multitude of antibiotics, including streptomycin, chloramphenicol, tetracycline, and erythromycin, among others.
- **Emergence of Antibiotic Resistance:** Despite their immense benefits, the overuse and misuse of antibiotics led to the emergence of antibiotic-resistant bacteria. This ongoing challenge underscores the importance of responsible antibiotic use and continued research into

new antimicrobial agents.

Nomenclature of Antibiotics: Antibiotics are classified based on various criteria, including their chemical structure, mechanism of action, and spectrum of activity. They are often named according to their source, mode of action, or chemical structure.

- **Source-based Nomenclature:** Many antibiotics are named based on the organism from which they are derived or the environment in which they are found. For example, penicillin is named after the Penicillium mold from which it was first isolated.
- **Mode of Action-based Nomenclature:** Some antibiotics are named according to their mechanism of action. For instance, bactericidal antibiotics kill bacteria, while bacteriostatic antibiotics inhibit bacterial growth.
- **Chemical Structure-based Nomenclature:** Antibiotics may also be named based on their chemical structure. This can include prefixes, suffixes, and stems that indicate specific functional groups or molecular features.

Stereochemistry of Antibiotics:
Stereochemistry refers to the three-dimensional arrangement of atoms in molecules and is crucial in determining the biological activity of antibiotics.

- **Chirality:** Many antibiotics contain chiral centers, which are carbon atoms bonded to four different groups. The arrangement of these groups in space gives rise to different stereoisomers, each with its own unique biological activity.

- **Enantiomers:** Enantiomers are mirror-image isomers that have the same chemical formula but differ in their spatial arrangement. In some cases, only one enantiomer of an antibiotic may exhibit antimicrobial activity, while the other may be inactive or even harmful.
- **Biological Activity:** The stereochemistry of antibiotics can profoundly influence their interactions with biological targets such as enzymes or bacterial cell walls. Small changes in stereochemistry can alter the efficacy, toxicity, and pharmacokinetic properties of antibiotics.

β-lactam antibiotics :- Penicillins

The most significant antibiotic, penicillin, was initially isolated from the mold Penicillium notatum. Penicillin is now produced commercially using a mutation of a similar mold called P. chrysogenum, which was later shown to provide the maximum output of the antibiotic. Penicillin is a member of the β-lactam antibiotic class of antibiotics. A thiazolidine ring united with a β-lactam ring makes up the fundamental structure of penicillins, which is necessary for their antibacterial activity. These two rings—6-amino penicillanic acid (6-APA)—make up the basic building block of all penicillins. By changing the makeup of the side chain connected to the 6-APA nucleus, a range of semi synthetic penicillins can be created. The side chain and nucleus of 6-APA are both necessary for the antibacterial action.

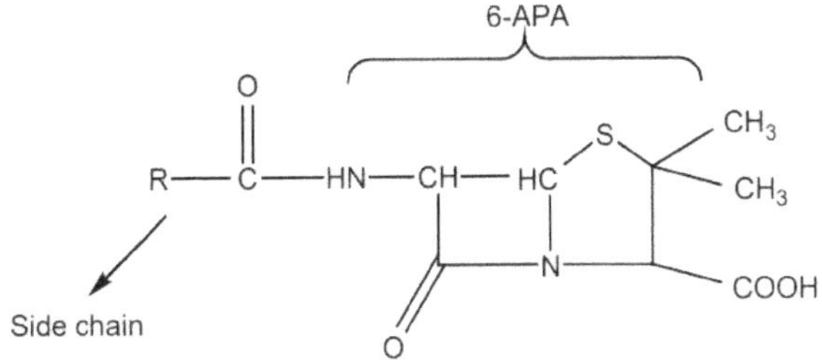

Basic structure of penicillin

• The penicillins are very reactive due to the strained amide bond in the fused β-lactum of the nucleus. • Penicillins undergo a complex series of reactions leading to a variety of inactive degradation products. Tahir99-VRG & vip.persianss.ir

• They are extremely susceptible to nucleophilic attack by water or hydroxide ion to form the penicilloic acid. β-Lactamses also cleave the β-lactam ring to give penicilloic acid with a consequent loss of antibacterial activity.

• In strongly acidic solutions (pH < 3), penicillin is protonated at the β-lactam nitrogen, and this is followed by nucleophillic attack of the acyl oxygen atom on the β-lactam carbonyl carbon. The subsequent opening of the β-lactam ring destabilizes the thiazoline ring, which opens to form penicillenic acid that degrades into two major products penicillamine and penilloic acid. A third product, penicilloaldehyde is also formed.

• Acid-catalyzed degradation in the stomach contributes in a major way to the poor oral absorption of penicillin. Thus, efforts to obtain penicillins with improved pharmacokinetic and microbiologic properties have sought to fi nd acyl functionalities that would minimize sensitivity of the β-lactam ring to acid hydrolysis and at the same time, maintain antibacterial activity.

• Substitution of an electron-withdrawing group for the α-position of the benzyl penicillin has stabilized the penicillin to acid catalyzed hydrolysis. The increased stability imparted by such electron-withdrawing groups has been attributed to a decrease in the reactivity of the side chain amide carbonyl oxygen atom towards participation in β-lactam ring opening to form the penicillenic acid.

Mode of action: The cell wall of bacteria is essential for the normal growth and development. Peptidoglycan is a heteropolymeric component of the cell wall that provides rigid mechanism for stability by virtue of its highly cross-linked lattice-wise structure. The peptidoglycan is composed of glycan chains, which are linear strands of two alternating amino sugars (N-acetyl glucosamine and N-acetylmuramic acid) that are cross-linked by peptide chains of an enzyme, transpeptidase. Penicillins inhibit the transpeptidase activity to the synthesis of cell walls.

Cephalosporins:

Antibiotics with Broad-Spectrum Efficacy

Cephalosporins represent a significant class of antibiotics renowned for their broad-spectrum activity against bacterial infections. Discovered in the 1940s by Italian pharmacologist Giuseppe Brotzu, cephalosporins have since become vital weapons in the medical arsenal against a wide range of pathogens. This article explores the historical background, mechanism of action, classification, and clinical significance of cephalosporins.

Historical Background:

Cephalosporins trace their origins to the fungus Acremonium (formerly Cephalosporium) acremonium, from which the cephalosporin C compound was first isolated. This breakthrough occurred in 1945 when Brotzu identified its potential as an antibacterial agent. However, it wasn't until the 1960s that the first cephalosporin antibiotic, cephalothin, was introduced for clinical use.

Mechanism of Action:

Cephalosporins exert their antimicrobial effects by inhibiting bacterial cell wall synthesis. Similar to penicillins, they contain a beta-lactam ring, which binds to penicillin-binding proteins (PBPs) located on the bacterial cell wall. This interaction disrupts the cross-linking of peptidoglycan, weakening the cell wall and leading to bacterial cell lysis and death.

Classification:

Cephalosporins are classified into generations based on their spectrum of activity and resistance to beta-lactamases, enzymes produced by bacteria to deactivate beta-lactam antibiotics. The classification includes:

1. **First Generation:** These cephalosporins are primarily effective against Gram-positive bacteria and some Gram-negative organisms. Examples include cephalexin and cefazolin.

2. **Second Generation:** Second-generation cephalosporins have increased activity against Gram-negative bacteria compared to first-generation drugs. They also exhibit extended coverage against some anaerobic bacteria. Examples include cefuroxime and cefoxitin.

3. **Third Generation:** Third-generation cephalosporins have enhanced activity against Gram-negative bacteria, including Enterobacteriaceae and Pseudomonas

aeruginosa. They also maintain efficacy against many Gram-positive organisms. Examples include ceftriaxone and cefotaxime.

4. **Fourth Generation:** Fourth-generation cephalosporins possess broad-spectrum activity against both Gram-positive and Gram-negative bacteria, including those resistant to earlier generations. Examples include cefepime and cefpirome.

5. **Fifth Generation:** Fifth-generation cephalosporins are the latest addition to the cephalosporin family. They exhibit enhanced activity against Gram-positive bacteria, including methicillin-resistant Staphylococcus aureus (MRSA), as well as some Gram-negative organisms. Examples include ceftaroline and ceftobiprole.

Clinical Significance:

Cephalosporins are widely used in clinical practice to treat various bacterial infections, including respiratory tract infections, urinary tract infections, skin and soft tissue infections, sepsis, and meningitis. Their broad-spectrum activity, low toxicity, and favorable safety profile make them valuable options for empirical therapy in many clinical scenarios.

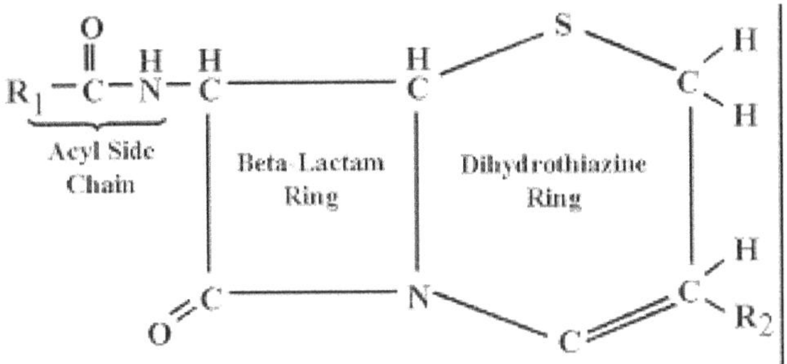

General Structure of Cephalosporins

Monobactams:

Unique Antibiotics Targeting Gram-Negative Bacteria

Monobactams represent a distinctive class of antibiotics renowned for their efficacy against Gram-negative bacteria. Their unique chemical structure and mechanism of action make them valuable therapeutic agents in the treatment of various bacterial infections. This article explores the history, mechanism of action, clinical uses, and significance of monobactams in modern medicine.

Historical Background:

Monobactams were first discovered in the late 1970s from the bacterium Chromobacterium violaceum. The prototype monobactam, aztreonam, was subsequently developed through chemical modification. It gained approval for clinical use in the United States in the early 1980s and has since become a vital component of the antibiotic armamentarium.

Mechanism of Action:

Monobactams, such as aztreonam, exert their antimicrobial effects by selectively targeting and inhibiting the activity of penicillin-binding protein 3 (PBP-3) in the bacterial cell wall synthesis process. Unlike other beta-lactam antibiotics, monobactams do not bind to other PBPs or cross-react with beta-lactamases, enzymes that can deactivate beta-lactam antibiotics. This unique mechanism of action confers excellent activity against Gram-negative bacteria, including Enterobacteriaceae, Pseudomonas aeruginosa, and some strains of Haemophilus influenzae.

Clinical Uses:

Monobactams are primarily indicated for the treatment of infections caused by susceptible Gram-negative bacteria, particularly in patients with allergies or sensitivities to other beta-lactam antibiotics, such as penicillins or cephalosporins. Aztreonam is commonly used to treat urinary tract infections, lower respiratory tract infections, intra-abdominal infections, skin and soft tissue infections, and sepsis caused by susceptible organisms.

Additionally, monobactams may play a role in combination therapy for the treatment of multidrug-resistant infections, particularly those involving Gram-negative bacteria resistant to other classes of antibiotics. The combination of aztreonam with beta-lactamase inhibitors or other antibiotics, such as aminoglycosides or fluoroquinolones, may enhance efficacy and overcome resistance mechanisms.

Significance in Modern Medicine:

Monobactams occupy a unique niche in the antibiotic armamentarium due to their selective activity against Gram-negative bacteria and favorable safety profile. Their ability to bypass common resistance mechanisms, such as beta-lactamase production and multidrug efflux pumps, makes them valuable therapeutic options in the era of increasing antibiotic resistance.

Furthermore, the development of new monobactam derivatives and combination therapies holds promise for expanding their clinical utility and addressing emerging resistance patterns. Ongoing research efforts are focused on optimizing the pharmacokinetic properties, spectrum of activity, and resistance profile of monobactams to enhance their effectiveness against a broader range of bacterial pathogens.

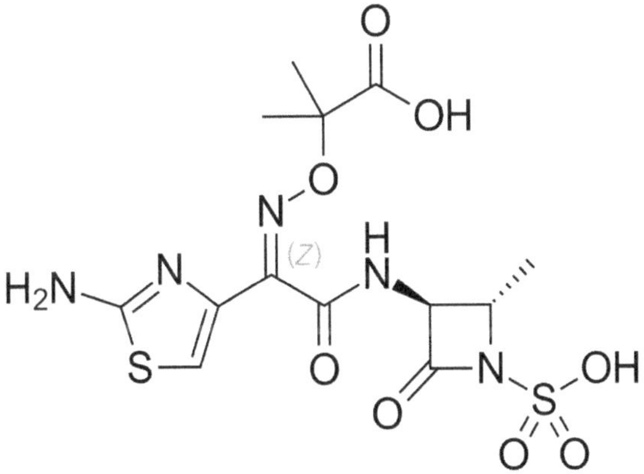

In conclusion, monobactams represent an important class of antibiotics with unique properties and clinical applications in the treatment of Gram-negative bacterial infections. Their distinct mechanism of action, selective activity, and potential for combination therapy make them indispensable tools in the fight against antibiotic-resistant bacteria and the management of infectious diseases in modern medicine.

Aminoglycosides: Aminoglycosides: Potent Antibiotics with Broad-Spectrum Activity

Aminoglycosides are a class of antibiotics known for their potent antimicrobial properties against a wide range of bacteria, including both Gram-positive and Gram-negative organisms. This article delves into the history, mechanism of action, clinical uses, and significance of aminoglycosides in modern medicine.

Historical Background:

The discovery of aminoglycosides dates back to the mid-20th century when researchers isolated streptomycin from Streptomyces griseus in 1943. Streptomycin marked the first effective treatment for tuberculosis and laid the foundation for the development of other aminoglycoside antibiotics, including neomycin, gentamicin, amikacin, and tobramycin, among others.

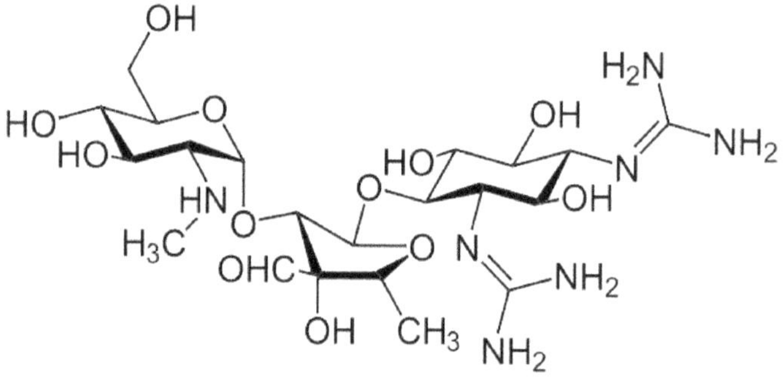

Mechanism of Action:

Aminoglycosides exert their antimicrobial effects by binding irreversibly to the bacterial 30S ribosomal subunit, thereby interfering with protein synthesis. This disruption leads to the misreading of mRNA and the production of faulty proteins, ultimately inhibiting bacterial growth and causing cell death. Additionally, aminoglycosides may disrupt bacterial cell membranes and induce the formation of reactive oxygen species, contributing to their bactericidal activity.

Clinical Uses:

Aminoglycosides are commonly used to treat severe and life-threatening infections caused by aerobic Gram-negative bacteria, such as Pseudomonas aeruginosa, Escherichia coli, Klebsiella pneumoniae, and Acinetobacter baumannii. They are particularly effective in treating infections of the urinary tract, respiratory tract, bloodstream, abdomen, skin, and soft tissues.

Additionally, aminoglycosides may be used in combination therapy for the treatment of certain Gram-positive infections, including endocarditis and osteomyelitis, when used in conjunction with beta-lactam antibiotics such as penicillins or cephalosporins. This combination therapy exploits synergistic effects to enhance antimicrobial efficacy and overcome resistance mechanisms.

Significance in Modern Medicine:

Despite their potent antimicrobial activity, aminoglycosides are associated with several significant limitations and potential adverse effects. These include nephrotoxicity (kidney damage), ototoxicity (hearing loss), neuromuscular blockade, and the emergence of bacterial resistance. To minimize these risks, aminoglycosides are typically administered in a dose-dependent manner and monitored closely to ensure therapeutic efficacy while minimizing toxicity.

Streptomycin: A Powerful Antibiotic Pioneer

Streptomycin stands as a beacon in the history of medicine, representing a monumental breakthrough in the treatment of bacterial infections. Discovered in 1943 by Selman Waksman and his team at Rutgers University, this antibiotic marked the dawn of a new era in the fight against diseases caused by bacteria.

Discovery and Development: Selman Waksman, along with his colleagues, unearthed Streptomycin from a soil-dwelling bacterium called Streptomyces griseus. This discovery was a result of extensive screening of soil microbes for antimicrobial properties, a process that revolutionized the field of pharmacology. Streptomycin's efficacy against tuberculosis, a disease that had plagued humanity for centuries, propelled it into the limelight of medical science.

Mechanism of Action: Streptomycin belongs to the class of antibiotics known as aminoglycosides. Its mechanism of action involves binding to the bacterial ribosome, specifically targeting the 30S subunit. By doing so, Streptomycin disrupts protein synthesis in bacteria, ultimately leading to cell death. This unique mode of action made it a formidable weapon against a wide array of bacterial infections.

Clinical Applications: Streptomycin's introduction heralded a turning point in the treatment of tuberculosis (TB), which was once a leading cause of mortality worldwide. Its efficacy in combating Mycobacterium tuberculosis, the causative agent of TB, rendered it an indispensable tool in the fight against this deadly disease. Additionally, Streptomycin found utility in treating other bacterial infections, including those caused by Escherichia coli, Salmonella, and various species of Mycobacterium.

Challenges and Limitations: Despite its remarkable efficacy, Streptomycin is not devoid of drawbacks. Prolonged use of this antibiotic can lead to the emergence of resistant bacterial strains, necessitating the development of alternative therapeutic strategies. Moreover, its use is associated with potential side effects, including ototoxicity and nephrotoxicity, which underscore the importance of judicious prescribing practices.

Legacy and Impact: The discovery of Streptomycin revolutionized the field of medicine, offering hope to millions afflicted by bacterial infections. Its success paved the way for the development of numerous other antibiotics, shaping the landscape of modern healthcare. Furthermore, Streptomycin served as a paradigm for subsequent drug discovery efforts, highlighting the untapped potential of natural sources in the quest for novel therapeutics.

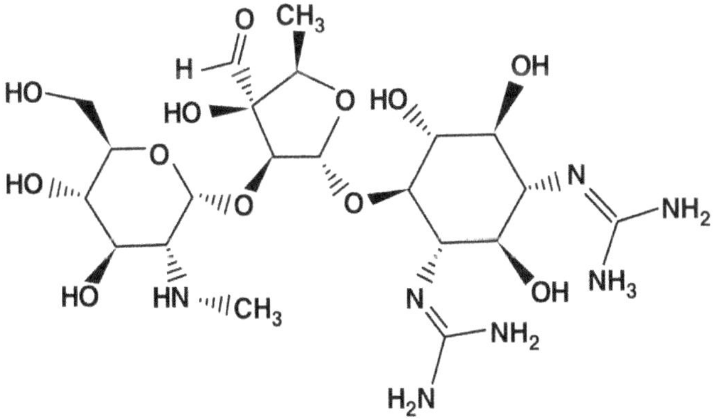

Neomycin stands as a stalwart in the arsenal of antibiotics, revered for its broad-spectrum antimicrobial activity and versatility in various medical and veterinary applications. Originally isolated from the soil bacterium Streptomyces fradiae in 1949, neomycin swiftly emerged as a potent therapeutic agent, demonstrating efficacy against a wide range of Gram-positive and Gram-negative bacteria.

Discovery and Development: Neomycin owes its discovery to the pioneering work of microbiologist Waksman and his team, who uncovered this antibiotic during their quest to unearth novel antimicrobial compounds from soil-dwelling microorganisms. Its identification marked a significant milestone in the field of pharmacology, offering new hope in the battle against infectious diseases.

Mechanism of Action: As an aminoglycoside antibiotic, neomycin operates by binding irreversibly to the 30S subunit of bacterial ribosomes, thereby disrupting protein synthesis. This interference with bacterial cellular machinery impairs essential functions, ultimately leading to bacterial cell death. Its mechanism of action makes it effective against a wide spectrum of bacterial pathogens.

Clinical Applications: Neomycin finds widespread use in clinical settings for the treatment and prevention of infections, particularly in topical formulations. It is commonly employed in combination with other antibiotics in ointments, creams, and powders to treat skin infections, wounds, and burns. Additionally, neomycin is utilized in oral formulations to treat gastrointestinal infections and as a preoperative prophylactic agent to reduce the risk of postoperative infections.

Veterinary Medicine: In veterinary medicine, neomycin plays a crucial role in safeguarding the health of livestock and pets. It is frequently included in medicated feed, oral solutions, and topical formulations to combat bacterial infections in animals. Neomycin's efficacy, coupled with its relatively low cost, has made it a staple in veterinary therapeutics for the prevention and treatment of bacterial diseases.

Challenges and Considerations: Despite its widespread use and effectiveness, neomycin is not without limitations. Prolonged use or systemic administration of neomycin can lead to the development of bacterial resistance and potential adverse effects, including nephrotoxicity and ototoxicity. Therefore, judicious prescribing practices and careful monitoring of patients are essential to mitigate these risks.

Kanamycin stands as a formidable member of the aminoglycoside class of antibiotics, renowned for its efficacy in combating a wide range of bacterial infections. Discovered in 1957 by Hamao Umezawa and his team in Japan, kanamycin swiftly earned recognition for its potent bactericidal properties and became an invaluable tool in the medical arsenal against infectious diseases.

Discovery and Development: The discovery of kanamycin emerged from the exploration of microbial biodiversity, with Umezawa's team isolating this antibiotic from Streptomyces kanamyceticus, a soil-dwelling bacterium. Its subsequent development marked a significant advancement in antibiotic research, offering new avenues for combating bacterial pathogens resistant to existing therapies.

Mechanism of Action: Kanamycin exerts its antimicrobial effects by binding irreversibly to the bacterial ribosome's 30S subunit, thereby disrupting protein synthesis. This interference with bacterial protein production halts essential cellular processes, ultimately leading to bacterial cell death. Its broad-spectrum activity encompasses both Gram-positive and Gram-negative bacteria, making it a versatile therapeutic agent.

Clinical Applications: Kanamycin finds widespread clinical use in treating various bacterial infections, particularly those caused by multidrug-resistant pathogens. It is commonly employed in the management of respiratory tract infections, urinary tract infections, gastrointestinal infections, and infections of the skin and soft tissues. Additionally, kanamycin is utilized in combination therapies for tuberculosis and other mycobacterial infections, demonstrating its efficacy against these challenging pathogens.

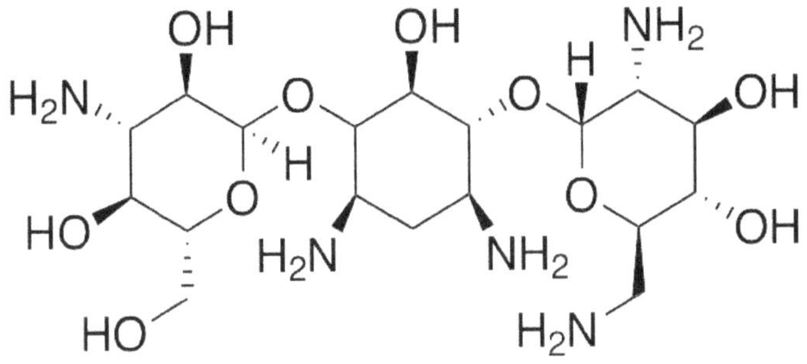

Tetracyclines: A Versatile Class of Antibiotics

Tetracyclines represent a class of broad-spectrum antibiotics that have played a pivotal role in combating bacterial infections since their discovery in the mid-20th century. With their unique mechanism of action and diverse clinical applications, tetracyclines have remained indispensable in modern medicine despite the emergence of newer antibiotic classes.

Discovery and Development: The discovery of tetracyclines traces back to the 1940s when Benjamin Minge Duggar identified chlortetracycline from the soil bacterium Streptomyces aureofaciens. This breakthrough paved the way for the subsequent isolation of other tetracyclines, including oxytetracycline and tetracycline itself. Over the decades, structural modifications and semi-synthetic derivatives have expanded the tetracycline family, enhancing their efficacy and pharmacokinetic properties.

Mechanism of Action: Tetracyclines exert their antibacterial effects by inhibiting bacterial protein synthesis. They bind reversibly to the bacterial ribosome's

30S subunit, preventing the attachment of aminoacyl-tRNA molecules to the ribosomal acceptor site. This interference disrupts the elongation of the polypeptide chain during protein synthesis, ultimately inhibiting bacterial growth and replication.

Clinical Applications: Tetracyclines find extensive clinical use in treating a wide array of bacterial infections, ranging from respiratory tract infections to sexually transmitted diseases. Their broad-spectrum activity encompasses Gram-positive and Gram-negative bacteria, as well as atypical pathogens such as Chlamydia, Mycoplasma, and Rickettsia. Common indications for tetracyclines include acne vulgaris, urinary tract infections, respiratory tract infections, Lyme disease, and certain sexually transmitted infections.

Challenges and Considerations: Despite their efficacy, tetracyclines are not without limitations. Prolonged or indiscriminate use can lead to the development of bacterial resistance, necessitating prudent prescribing practices and antimicrobial stewardship. Additionally, tetracyclines are contraindicated in pregnant women and children due to potential adverse effects on tooth development and bone growth. Moreover, they may cause gastrointestinal upset, photosensitivity, and allergic reactions in susceptible individuals.

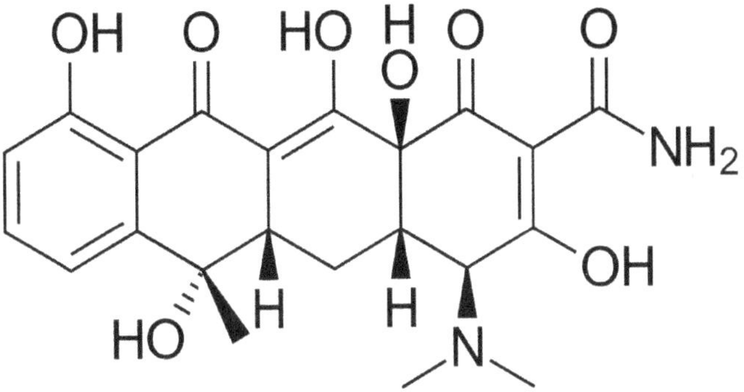

Oxytetracycline, a member of the tetracycline class of antibiotics, has long been revered for its broad-spectrum antimicrobial activity and versatility in medical, veterinary, and agricultural settings. Since its discovery in the 1940s, oxytetracycline has remained a cornerstone in the fight against bacterial infections, demonstrating efficacy against a wide range of pathogens.

Discovery and Development: Oxytetracycline was first isolated from the soil bacterium Streptomyces rimosus by Alexander Finlay and his colleagues in 1948. This discovery marked a significant milestone in antibiotic research, offering a potent therapeutic agent against bacterial infections. Subsequent refinements and modifications have led to the development of semi-synthetic derivatives with enhanced pharmacokinetic properties and efficacy.

Mechanism of Action: Oxytetracycline exerts its antimicrobial effects by inhibiting bacterial protein synthesis. Similar to other tetracyclines, it binds reversibly to the bacterial ribosome's 30S subunit, preventing the attachment of aminoacyl-tRNA molecules to the ribosomal acceptor site. This interference disrupts protein synthesis, ultimately halting bacterial growth and replication.

Clinical Applications: Oxytetracycline finds widespread clinical use in treating various bacterial infections in humans. It is commonly prescribed for respiratory tract infections, urinary tract infections, skin and soft tissue infections, and sexually transmitted diseases. Additionally, oxytetracycline is utilized in the management of acne vulgaris, rosacea, and other dermatological conditions due to its anti-inflammatory properties.

Veterinary and Agricultural Uses: In veterinary medicine, oxytetracycline plays a crucial role in preventing and treating bacterial infections in livestock and companion animals. It is commonly administered orally or parenterally to combat respiratory infections, enteric infections, mastitis, and reproductive tract infections in animals. Moreover, oxytetracycline is utilized prophylactically in agriculture to promote animal growth and prevent bacterial diseases in livestock and poultry.

Chlortetracycline, a member of the tetracycline class of antibiotics, has long been recognized for its potent antimicrobial properties and diverse applications in human and veterinary medicine. Since its discovery in the mid-20th century, chlortetracycline has remained an essential tool in combating bacterial infections and promoting animal health and productivity.

Discovery and Development: Chlortetracycline was first isolated from the soil bacterium Streptomyces aureofaciens in 1948 by American microbiologist Benjamin Minge Duggar. This discovery marked a significant breakthrough in antibiotic research, offering a novel therapeutic agent against a broad spectrum of bacterial pathogens. Subsequent research efforts led to the development of semi-synthetic derivatives with enhanced pharmacokinetic properties and efficacy.

Mechanism of Action: Chlortetracycline exerts its antimicrobial effects by inhibiting bacterial protein synthesis. Like other tetracyclines, it binds reversibly to the bacterial ribosome's 30S subunit, interfering with the attachment of aminoacyl-tRNA molecules to the ribosomal acceptor site. This disruption halts protein synthesis, ultimately arresting bacterial growth and replication.

Clinical Applications: Chlortetracycline finds widespread clinical use in treating various bacterial infections in humans. It is commonly prescribed for respiratory tract infections, urinary tract infections, skin and soft tissue infections, and sexually transmitted diseases. Additionally, chlortetracycline is utilized in the management of acne vulgaris, rosacea, and other dermatological conditions due to its anti-inflammatory properties.

Veterinary Uses: In veterinary medicine, chlortetracycline plays a crucial role in promoting animal health and productivity. It is commonly administered orally or parenterally to prevent and treat bacterial infections in livestock and poultry. Chlortetracycline is particularly valuable in the control of respiratory diseases, enteric infections, mastitis, and reproductive tract infections in animals.

Agricultural Applications: Chlortetracycline is also employed prophylactically in agriculture to promote animal growth and prevent bacterial diseases in livestock and poultry. It is often incorporated into animal feed or administered in drinking water to control bacterial infections and enhance feed efficiency. Moreover, chlortetracycline is utilized in aquaculture to prevent and treat bacterial diseases in fish and other aquatic organisms.

Minocycline, a member of the tetracycline class of antibiotics, has emerged as a versatile therapeutic agent renowned for its broad-spectrum antimicrobial activity and diverse clinical applications. Since its introduction in the 1960s, minocycline has played a pivotal role in the management of various bacterial infections and inflammatory conditions, offering a potent and well-tolerated treatment option.

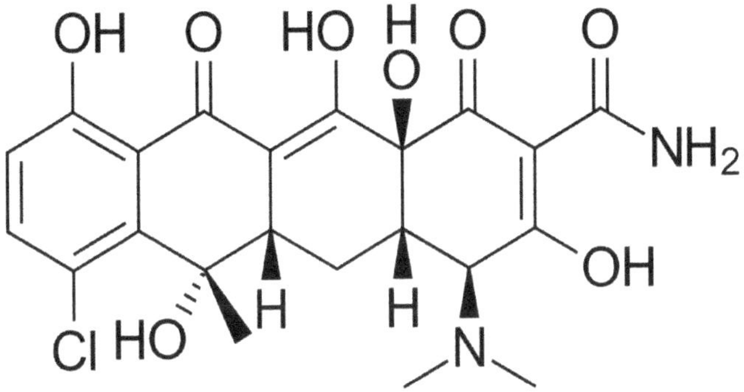

Discovery and Development: Minocycline was first synthesized in the early 1960s through chemical modification of the parent compound tetracycline. This structural alteration endowed minocycline with enhanced lipophilicity and tissue penetration, resulting in improved pharmacokinetic properties and efficacy compared to other tetracyclines. Its introduction marked a significant advancement in antibiotic therapy, offering a potent and versatile agent against a wide range of bacterial pathogens.

Mechanism of Action: Minocycline exerts its antimicrobial effects by inhibiting bacterial protein synthesis. Similar to other tetracyclines, it binds reversibly to the bacterial ribosome's 30S subunit, preventing the attachment of aminoacyl-tRNA molecules to the ribosomal acceptor site. This interference disrupts protein synthesis, ultimately inhibiting bacterial growth and replication. Additionally, minocycline exhibits anti-inflammatory and immunomodulatory properties, contributing to its therapeutic efficacy in non-infectious conditions.

Clinical Applications: Minocycline finds extensive clinical use in treating various bacterial infections in humans. It is commonly prescribed for respiratory tract infections, urinary tract infections, skin and soft tissue infections, and sexually transmitted diseases. Additionally, minocycline is utilized in the management of acne vulgaris, rosacea, and other dermatological conditions due to its anti-inflammatory properties. Moreover, minocycline is effective against atypical bacterial pathogens, making it a valuable agent in the treatment of infections such as Lyme disease and Mycoplasma pneumoniae pneumonia.

Neurological and Rheumatological Conditions: Beyond its antimicrobial properties, minocycline has demonstrated therapeutic efficacy in neurological and rheumatological disorders. Studies have suggested its potential neuroprotective effects in neurodegenerative diseases such as Parkinson's disease and Alzheimer's disease. Additionally, minocycline has shown promise in the treatment of autoimmune conditions like rheumatoid arthritis and multiple sclerosis, owing to its anti-inflammatory and immunomodulatory actions.

Doxycycline, a member of the tetracycline class of antibiotics, holds a prominent place in modern medicine due to its broad-spectrum antimicrobial activity and diverse therapeutic applications. Since its introduction in the 1960s, doxycycline has proven to be an indispensable tool in the management of bacterial infections, inflammatory conditions, and beyond.

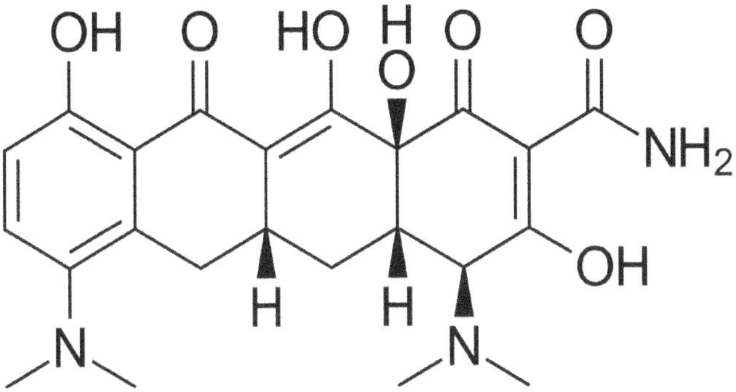

Discovery and Development: Doxycycline was developed through chemical modification of the parent compound tetracycline to improve its pharmacokinetic properties and efficacy. This modification endowed doxycycline with enhanced lipophilicity and tissue penetration, resulting in improved bioavailability and longer half-life compared to other tetracyclines. Its introduction marked a significant milestone in antibiotic therapy, offering a potent and versatile agent against a wide range of bacterial pathogens.

Mechanism of Action: Doxycycline exerts its antimicrobial effects by inhibiting bacterial protein synthesis. Like other tetracyclines, it binds reversibly to the bacterial ribosome's 30S subunit, preventing the attachment of aminoacyl-tRNA molecules to the ribosomal acceptor site. This interference disrupts protein synthesis, ultimately inhibiting bacterial growth and replication. Additionally, doxycycline exhibits anti-inflammatory and immunomodulatory properties, contributing to its therapeutic efficacy in non-infectious conditions.

Clinical Applications: Doxycycline finds extensive clinical use in treating various bacterial infections in humans. It is commonly prescribed for respiratory tract infections, urinary tract infections, skin and soft tissue infections, and sexually transmitted diseases. Additionally, doxycycline is utilized in the management of acne vulgaris, rosacea, and other dermatological conditions due to its anti-inflammatory properties. Moreover, doxycycline is effective against atypical bacterial pathogens, making it a valuable agent in the treatment of infections such as Lyme disease, chlamydia, and Mycoplasma pneumoniae pneumonia.

Malaria Prophylaxis and Treatment: Doxycycline is also used for malaria prophylaxis and treatment. It is particularly valuable in regions where chloroquine-resistant Plasmodium species are prevalent. Its efficacy, tolerability, and convenient dosing regimen make it a preferred choice for travelers to malaria-endemic areas.

Dental and Periodontal Conditions: In dentistry, doxycycline is utilized in the management of dental infections and periodontal diseases. It is often prescribed as an adjunctive therapy for the treatment of periodontitis and peri-implantitis due to its antimicrobial and anti-inflammatory properties.

UNIT – II
Antibiotics

The discovery and development of antibiotics represent one of the most significant advancements in medical science, revolutionizing the treatment of bacterial infections and saving countless lives. The historical journey of antibiotics spans centuries, marked by serendipitous discoveries, pioneering research, and transformative breakthroughs.

Early Observations: The concept of using natural substances to combat infectious diseases dates back thousands of years, with ancient civilizations employing various plant extracts, molds, and other remedies for their antimicrobial properties. Historical records from ancient Egypt, Greece, and China document the use of honey, garlic, and other natural substances to treat wounds and infections.

The Age of Antiseptics: In the 19th century, the pioneering work of figures such as Ignaz Semmelweis and Joseph Lister laid the foundation for modern infection control practices. Semmelweis advocated for hand hygiene to prevent childbirth fever, while Lister introduced antiseptic techniques using carbolic acid to sterilize surgical instruments and wounds. These practices marked a significant step forward in reducing the incidence of infections in healthcare settings.

The Era of Antibiotic Discovery: The true dawn of antibiotics began in the early 20th century, with the groundbreaking discovery of lysozyme by Alexander Fleming in 1928. Fleming's serendipitous observation of bacterial inhibition by a mold contaminant led to the discovery of penicillin, the first true antibiotic. Fleming's work laid the groundwork for the subsequent development of penicillin as a therapeutic agent by Howard Florey, Ernst Boris Chain, and Norman Heatley.

Penicillin and Beyond: The mass production of penicillin during World War II transformed the treatment of bacterial infections, saving countless lives and ushering in the antibiotic era. The success of penicillin spurred intensive research into other antimicrobial agents, leading to the discovery of streptomycin, chloramphenicol, tetracyclines, and other classes of antibiotics in subsequent decades.

Golden Age of Antibiotics: The period from the 1940s to the 1960s is often referred to as the "Golden Age" of antibiotics, characterized by a rapid expansion in the discovery, development, and clinical use of antimicrobial agents. This era saw the introduction of a plethora of antibiotics targeting a wide range of bacterial pathogens, transforming the landscape of infectious disease management.

Challenges and Resurgence: However, the indiscriminate use of antibiotics, coupled with the emergence of antibiotic-resistant bacteria, posed new challenges to public health. In recent decades, there has been a resurgence of interest in antibiotic discovery and development, driven by the urgent need for novel antimicrobial agents to combat multidrug-resistant pathogens.

Nomenclature and Stereochemistry in Chemistry

Nomenclature and stereochemistry are fundamental aspects of chemistry, playing crucial roles in accurately describing and understanding the structures and properties of molecules. These principles provide a systematic framework for naming chemical compounds and elucidating their three-dimensional arrangements, respectively, thereby facilitating communication and comprehension within the scientific community.

Nomenclature:

Nomenclature, or the naming of chemical compounds, follows standardized rules established by international organizations such as the International Union of Pure and Applied Chemistry (IUPAC). This systematic approach ensures clarity, consistency, and precision in the naming process, allowing chemists worldwide to communicate effectively.

Key principles of nomenclature include:

1. **Functional Groups:** The presence of specific functional groups within a compound often dictates its nomenclature. For example, compounds containing an alcohol functional group are named with the suffix "-ol," while those with a carboxylic acid group are named with the suffix "-oic acid."

2. **Parent Chain:** In organic compounds, the longest continuous carbon chain serves as the parent chain, with substituents attached to it indicated by prefixes and numerical locants.

3. **Substituents:** Alkyl groups and other substituents are named based on the number of carbon atoms they contain, with prefixes such as "methyl," "ethyl," and "propyl" denoting specific alkyl groups.

4. **Stereoisomers:** Compounds exhibiting stereoisomerism, such as geometric isomers and optical isomers, are distinguished by prefixes like "cis-" and "trans-" for geometric isomers and "D-" and "L-" for optical isomers.

5. **Functional Group Priority:** In cases where multiple functional groups are present, priority rules are applied to determine the primary functional group for naming purposes.

Stereochemistry:

Stereochemistry is the branch of chemistry concerned with the three-dimensional arrangement of atoms within molecules and the spatial relationships between molecules. It encompasses the study of stereoisomers, which are molecules with the same molecular formula and connectivity but differing in their spatial arrangement.

Key concepts in stereochemistry include:

1. **Chirality:** Chiral molecules are non-superimposable mirror images of each other, known as enantiomers. Chirality arises from the presence of an asymmetric carbon atom, also known as a chiral center, which is bonded to four different substituents.

2. **Enantiomers and Diastereomers:** Enantiomers are pairs of molecules that are mirror images of each other and exhibit optical activity. Diastereomers, on the other hand, are stereoisomers that are not mirror images and may have different physical and chemical properties.

3. **Stereoisomerism:** Stereoisomers can arise from geometric variations (cis-trans isomerism) or spatial arrangements around double bonds (E-Z isomerism) and asymmetric centers (R/S configuration).

4. **Conformational Isomers:** Conformational isomers are different spatial arrangements of the same molecule that result from rotation around single bonds. These isomers are typically interconvertible at room temperature and do not constitute distinct chemical entities.

Macrolides: A Cornerstone in Antibiotic Therapy

Macrolides represent a class of antibiotics renowned for their broad-spectrum activity against a wide range of bacterial pathogens. These versatile drugs have played a pivotal role in the treatment of various infectious diseases since their discovery, offering efficacy, tolerability, and a favorable safety profile. Let's delve into the characteristics, mechanisms of action, clinical uses, and considerations associated with macrolide antibiotics.

Characteristics of Macrolides:

Macrolides derive their name from their macrocyclic lactone chemical structure, which typically consists of a large lactone ring with attached sugar moieties. The most commonly used macrolides include erythromycin, azithromycin, clarithromycin, and dirithromycin. They are primarily bacteriostatic but can exhibit bactericidal activity at higher concentrations or against certain bacterial strains.

Mechanism of Action:

Macrolides exert their antimicrobial effects by binding to the bacterial ribosome's 50S subunit, thereby inhibiting protein synthesis. This interference prevents the elongation of the polypeptide chain during translation, ultimately halting bacterial growth and replication. Macrolides are particularly effective against Gram-positive bacteria but also demonstrate activity against some Gram-negative and atypical pathogens.

Clinical Uses:

Macrolide antibiotics find extensive clinical use in the treatment of various bacterial infections, including respiratory tract infections, skin and soft tissue infections, and sexually transmitted diseases. They are often preferred for patients with penicillin allergies or intolerances. Azithromycin, with its convenient once-daily dosing and shorter treatment duration, is frequently prescribed for respiratory infections, including community-acquired pneumonia and acute exacerbations of chronic obstructive pulmonary disease (COPD).

Clarithromycin and erythromycin are commonly used in the treatment of Helicobacter pylori infection associated with peptic ulcer disease and gastritis. Additionally, macrolides possess anti-inflammatory and immuno modulatory properties, making them useful adjuncts in the management of chronic inflammatory conditions such as cystic fibrosis and bronchiectasis.

Considerations and Adverse Effects:

While generally well-tolerated, macrolide antibiotics can cause adverse effects, including gastrointestinal symptoms (nausea, vomiting, diarrhea), hepatotoxicity, and QT interval prolongation, particularly with erythromycin. Additionally, macrolides may interact with other medications, such as statins and anticoagulants, increasing the risk of adverse drug reactions.

Emerging Challenges:

The emergence of bacterial resistance poses a significant challenge to the continued efficacy of macrolide antibiotics. Efflux pumps, ribosomal modifications, and enzymatic inactivation mechanisms contribute to macrolide resistance among bacterial pathogens. Consequently, judicious use and antimicrobial stewardship are crucial to mitigate the spread of resistance and preserve the effectiveness of these valuable antibiotics.

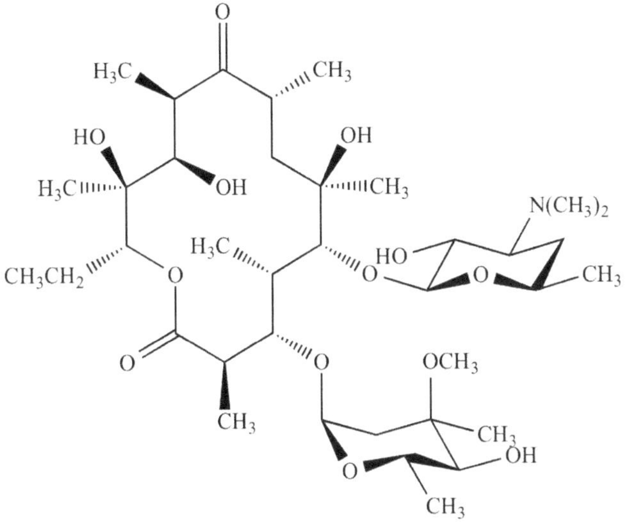

Erythromycin: A Versatile Antibiotic for Infectious Diseases

Erythromycin, a member of the macrolide class of antibiotics, stands as a cornerstone in the treatment of bacterial infections. Since its discovery, erythromycin has been widely prescribed for its broad-spectrum activity, efficacy, and tolerability, making it a valuable therapeutic agent across various medical specialties. Let's explore the characteristics, mechanism of action, clinical uses, and considerations associated with erythromycin.

Characteristics of Erythromycin:

Erythromycin is a macrolide antibiotic characterized by its macrocyclic lactone ring structure. It is derived from the soil bacterium Streptomyces erythreus and exhibits bacteriostatic activity against a broad spectrum of Gram-positive bacteria, including Streptococcus pneumoniae,

Staphylococcus aureus, and Corynebacterium diphtheriae. Erythromycin is particularly useful in patients with penicillin allergies or intolerances.

Mechanism of Action:

Erythromycin exerts its antimicrobial effects by binding to the bacterial ribosome's 50S subunit, thereby inhibiting protein synthesis. By preventing the elongation of the polypeptide chain during translation, erythromycin effectively halts bacterial growth and replication. This mechanism of action makes erythromycin effective against a variety of bacterial pathogens, including those causing respiratory tract infections, skin and soft tissue infections, and sexually transmitted diseases.

Clinical Uses:

Erythromycin finds widespread clinical use in the treatment of various bacterial infections. It is commonly prescribed for respiratory tract infections such as community-acquired pneumonia, bronchitis, and pertussis. Erythromycin is also effective against skin and soft tissue infections, including cellulitis and impetigo, as well as sexually transmitted infections such as chlamydia and syphilis.

In addition to its antimicrobial properties, erythromycin possesses prokinetic effects on the gastrointestinal tract, making it useful in the management of gastroparesis and other motility disorders. Erythromycin is also employed as an alternative or adjunctive therapy in the treatment of gastrointestinal infections caused by Campylobacter jejuni and Helicobacter pylori.

Considerations and Adverse Effects:

While generally well-tolerated, erythromycin can cause adverse effects, particularly gastrointestinal symptoms such as nausea, vomiting, and diarrhea.

Hepatotoxicity and QT interval prolongation are rare but potentially serious adverse effects associated with erythromycin use. Additionally, erythromycin may interact with other medications, such as statins and anticoagulants, increasing the risk of adverse drug reactions.

Emerging Challenges:

The emergence of bacterial resistance poses a significant challenge to the continued efficacy of erythromycin and other macrolide antibiotics. Efflux pumps, ribosomal modifications, and enzymatic inactivation mechanisms contribute to erythromycin resistance among bacterial pathogens. Consequently, judicious use and antimicrobial stewardship are crucial to mitigate the spread of resistance and preserve the effectiveness of erythromycin.

Clarithromycin: A Potent Macrolide Antibiotic

Clarithromycin, a semi-synthetic derivative of erythromycin, belongs to the macrolide class of antibiotics. Known for its broad-spectrum antimicrobial activity and favorable pharmacokinetic profile, clarithromycin has become a cornerstone in the treatment of various bacterial infections. Let's explore the characteristics, mechanism of action, clinical uses, and considerations associated with clarithromycin.

Characteristics of Clarithromycin:

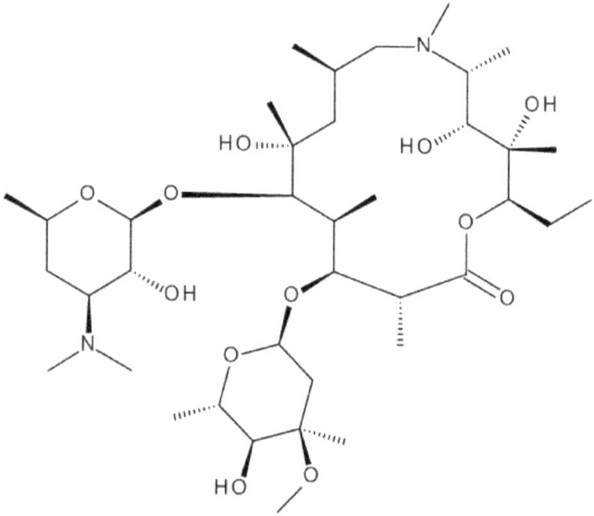

Clarithromycin possesses a macrocyclic lactone ring structure similar to erythromycin, with modifications that confer improved pharmacokinetic properties and enhanced activity against certain bacterial pathogens. These modifications include the addition of a 14-membered lactone ring and methyl groups at positions 6 and 11 of the lactone ring. These structural alterations enhance clarithromycin's stability, bioavailability, and tissue penetration compared to erythromycin.

Mechanism of Action:

Clarithromycin exerts its antimicrobial effects by binding to the bacterial ribosome's 50S subunit, thereby inhibiting protein synthesis. This interference disrupts bacterial growth and replication, ultimately leading to bacteriostasis. Clarithromycin demonstrates broad-spectrum activity against Gram-positive bacteria, including Streptococcus pneumoniae, Staphylococcus aureus, and atypical pathogens such as Mycoplasma pneumoniae and Legionella pneumophila.

Clinical Uses:

Clarithromycin is indicated for the treatment of various bacterial infections across multiple medical specialties. It is commonly prescribed for respiratory tract infections, including community-acquired pneumonia, acute exacerbations of chronic bronchitis, and sinusitis. Clarithromycin is also effective against skin and soft tissue infections, Helicobacter pylori-associated peptic ulcer disease, and certain sexually transmitted infections such as chlamydia.

In addition to its antimicrobial properties, clarithromycin possesses immunomodulatory effects, making it useful in the management of chronic inflammatory conditions such as chronic obstructive pulmonary disease (COPD) exacerbations and diffuse panbronchiolitis. Clarithromycin's ability to reduce airway inflammation and mucus production contributes to its therapeutic efficacy in these conditions.

Considerations and Adverse Effects:

While generally well-tolerated, clarithromycin can cause adverse effects, including gastrointestinal symptoms such as nausea, vomiting, and diarrhea. Hepatotoxicity, QT interval prolongation, and allergic reactions are rare but potentially serious adverse effects associated with clarithromycin use. Clinicians should exercise caution when prescribing clarithromycin to patients with pre-existing hepatic impairment or cardiac conduction abnormalities.

Emerging Challenges:

As with other antibiotics, the emergence of bacterial resistance poses a significant challenge to the continued efficacy of clarithromycin. Efflux pumps, ribosomal modifications, and enzymatic inactivation mechanisms contribute to clarithromycin resistance among bacterial pathogens. Consequently, judicious use and antimicrobial stewardship are crucial to mitigate the spread of resistance and preserve the effectiveness of clarithromycin.

Azithromycin Introduction: Azithromycin is a widely-used antibiotic belonging to the macrolide class, known for its efficacy in treating a variety of bacterial infections. Whether its respiratory tract infections, skin infections, or sexually transmitted diseases, azithromycin has become a cornerstone in the arsenal of antibiotics. This article delves into the uses, benefits, and considerations surrounding azithromycin.

Uses:

1. **Respiratory Tract Infections**: Azithromycin is commonly prescribed for respiratory infections such as bronchitis, pneumonia, and sinusitis. Its broad-spectrum activity against bacteria makes it effective in combating these infections.
2. **Skin and Soft Tissue Infections**: From mild to moderate cases of cellulitis, impetigo, or folliculitis, azithromycin proves beneficial due to its ability to penetrate skin tissues effectively.
3. **Sexually Transmitted Infections (STIs)**: Azithromycin is often prescribed as part of the treatment regimen for STIs like chlamydia and gonorrhea. Its single-dose regimen makes it convenient for patients and healthcare providers alike.
4. **Ophthalmic Infections**: Azithromycin is also available

in ophthalmic formulations for treating bacterial conjunctivitis, providing a localized treatment option for eye infections.

Benefits:

1. **Convenience**: Azithromycin's extended half-life allows for less frequent dosing, making it a convenient option for patients, particularly in the treatment of STIs where single-dose regimens are effective.
2. **Broader Spectrum**: Compared to some other antibiotics, azithromycin offers a broader spectrum of activity against various bacteria, which enhances its utility in treating a range of infections.
3. **Well-Tolerated**: Azithromycin is generally well-tolerated, with fewer gastrointestinal side effects compared to other antibiotics in its class, making it suitable for patients with sensitive stomachs.
4. **Minimal Drug Interactions**: Azithromycin has fewer interactions with other medications compared to some other antibiotics, reducing the risk of complications in patients with multiple medication regimens.

Considerations:

1. **Antibiotic Resistance**: As with all antibiotics, the overuse or misuse of azithromycin can contribute to the development of antibiotic resistance. It's crucial to use this medication responsibly and only as prescribed by a healthcare professional.
2. **Side Effects**: While generally well-tolerated, azithromycin can cause side effects such as gastrointestinal disturbances (nausea, diarrhea),

headaches, and allergic reactions in some individuals. Patients should be aware of these potential side effects and report any adverse reactions to their healthcare provider.

3. **Precautions**: Azithromycin may not be suitable for everyone, especially those with pre-existing liver conditions or certain heart rhythm disorders. It's important for healthcare providers to assess each patient's medical history before prescribing azithromycin.

4. **Pregnancy and Lactation**: The safety of azithromycin during pregnancy and lactation is not fully established. Healthcare providers weigh the potential risks and benefits before prescribing azithromycin to pregnant or breastfeeding individuals.

Chloramphenicol: Chloramphenicol is an antibiotic medication that has been an essential tool in the fight against bacterial infections for decades. Its broad spectrum of activity makes it effective against a wide range of bacterial pathogens, making it invaluable in certain clinical scenarios. However, its usage is tempered by its potential for serious side effects, necessitating careful consideration by healthcare professionals.

Uses: Chloramphenicol is primarily used to treat bacterial infections caused by susceptible organisms. These infections may include:

1. **Typhoid Fever:** Chloramphenicol has historically been a mainstay in the treatment of typhoid fever, a systemic illness caused by Salmonella typhi.

2. **Bacterial Meningitis:** It is effective against certain strains of bacteria that cause meningitis, a potentially

life-threatening infection of the membranes covering the brain and spinal cord.

3. **Respiratory Tract Infections:** Chloramphenicol can be used to treat respiratory infections caused by susceptible organisms, such as Haemophilus influenzae and Streptococcus pneumoniae.
4. **Other Infections:** It may also be used to treat other bacterial infections when other antibiotics are not suitable or available.

Mechanism of Action: Chloramphenicol exerts its antibacterial effects by inhibiting bacterial protein synthesis. Specifically, it binds reversibly to the 50S subunit of the bacterial ribosome, thereby preventing the formation of peptide bonds between amino acids during translation. This interference with protein synthesis disrupts bacterial growth and replication, ultimately leading to bacterial cell death or inhibition of growth.

Risks and Side Effects: Despite its effectiveness, chloramphenicol is associated with significant risks, particularly hematologic toxicity. The most serious adverse effect is bone marrow suppression, which can manifest as aplastic anemia, agranulocytosis, or thrombocytopenia. These conditions can be life-threatening and may necessitate discontinuation of the medication. Due to these risks, chloramphenicol should be used cautiously and reserved for situations where its benefits outweigh the potential harms.

Other common side effects of chloramphenicol may include:

- **Gastrointestinal Disturbances:** Nausea, vomiting, and diarrhea are relatively common side effects.
- **Allergic Reactions:** Some individuals may experience allergic reactions, ranging from mild rashes to severe anaphylaxis.
- **Gray Baby Syndrome:** In newborns and premature infants, chloramphenicol can cause "gray baby syndrome," characterized by cyanosis, abdominal distension, cardiovascular collapse, and grayish discoloration of the skin.

Clindamycin is a potent antibiotic medication that plays a crucial role in the treatment of various bacterial infections. Its broad-spectrum activity and ability to penetrate tissues make it effective against a wide range of pathogens. However, like all antibiotics, its use should be guided by careful consideration of the infection type, susceptibility patterns, and potential side effects.

Uses: Clindamycin is prescribed for the treatment of both Gram-positive and Gram-negative bacterial infections.

Some common indications for its use include:

1. **Skin and Soft Tissue Infections:** Clindamycin is often used to treat skin infections such as cellulitis, abscesses, and infected wounds caused by susceptible bacteria.
2. **Bone and Joint Infections:** It may be used as part of the treatment regimen for bone and joint infections, including osteomyelitis and septic arthritis.
3. **Intra-abdominal Infections:** Clindamycin can be effective in treating intra-abdominal infections such as peritonitis and intra-abdominal abscesses.
4. **Respiratory Tract Infections:** It is sometimes used to treat respiratory infections caused by susceptible organisms, including certain strains of Streptococcus pneumoniae and anaerobic bacteria.
5. **Gynecological Infections:** Clindamycin may be prescribed for the treatment of gynecological infections such as pelvic inflammatory disease (PID) and bacterial vaginosis.

Mechanism of Action: Clindamycin belongs to the lincosamide class of antibiotics and acts by inhibiting bacterial protein synthesis. It binds to the 50S subunit of the bacterial ribosome, blocking the translocation step of protein synthesis. This disruption in protein production ultimately leads to bacterial cell death or inhibition of growth.

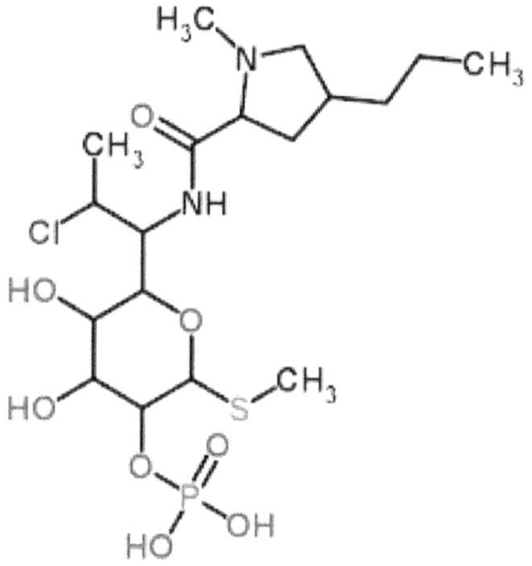

Risks and Side Effects: While generally well-tolerated, clindamycin, like other antibiotics, can cause side effects. Common side effects may include:

- **Gastrointestinal Upset:** Nausea, vomiting, diarrhea, and abdominal pain are among the most frequently reported side effects. Pseudomembranous colitis, a severe form of antibiotic-associated diarrhea, can also occur, sometimes leading to life-threatening complications.
- **Allergic Reactions:** Some individuals may experience allergic reactions, ranging from mild rashes to severe anaphylaxis. Patients with a history of allergic reactions to clindamycin or other antibiotics should be closely monitored.
- **Rare but Serious Side Effects:** Clindamycin has been associated with rare but potentially severe side effects, including severe skin reactions (such as Stevens-Johnson syndrome and toxic epidermal necrolysis),

hepatotoxicity, and blood disorders.

Prodrugs: Enhancing Drug Delivery and Efficacy

Introduction: Prodrugs represent a clever strategy in pharmacology where a pharmacologically inactive compound is administered, which undergoes chemical or enzymatic transformation in the body to produce the active drug. This approach offers several advantages in terms of drug delivery, efficacy, and patient tolerance.

How Prodrugs Work: Prodrugs are designed to overcome limitations associated with the parent drug, such as poor solubility, stability, or bioavailability. By modifying the chemical structure of the drug molecule, it becomes inactive or less active, allowing for improved handling and delivery. Once inside the body, prodrugs undergo specific chemical or enzymatic reactions to convert into the active form of the drug.

Types of Prodrugs:

1. **Ester Prodrugs:** Esterification involves linking the active drug molecule to an ester moiety, which is easily hydrolyzed by esterases in the body to release the active compound. Common examples include aspirin and certain antiviral medications.

2. **Phosphate Prodrugs:** Phosphate prodrugs involve the addition of a phosphate group to the drug molecule, enhancing its water solubility and bioavailability. Once inside the body, phosphatases cleave the phosphate group to release the active drug. This approach is utilized in some antiviral and anticancer agents.

3. **Amide Prodrugs:** Amide prodrugs involve the addition of an amide group to the drug molecule, which is subsequently hydrolyzed by amidases to release the

active drug. This strategy is employed in some antibiotics and analgesics.

4. **Bioprecursor Prodrugs:** Bioprecursor prodrugs are designed to undergo metabolic conversion in the body to yield the active drug. This approach allows for the generation of active metabolites with improved pharmacokinetic properties.

Advantages of Prodrugs:

1. **Improved Bioavailability:** Prodrugs can enhance the absorption of poorly soluble drugs, leading to improved bioavailability and therapeutic efficacy.
2. **Reduced Side Effects:** By targeting drug delivery to specific sites or tissues, prodrugs can minimize systemic exposure and reduce the risk of adverse effects.
3. **Enhanced Stability:** Prodrugs can protect the active drug from degradation or metabolism, increasing its stability in biological fluids.
4. **Site-Specific Targeting:** Prodrugs can be designed to target specific tissues or cells, allowing for localized drug delivery and improved therapeutic outcomes.

Examples of Prodrugs:

1. **Valacyclovir:** This prodrug of acyclovir is used in the treatment of herpes simplex and varicella-zoster infections. Once absorbed, valacyclovir is rapidly converted to acyclovir by esterases in the liver.
2. **Enalapril:** Enalapril is a prodrug of enalaprilat, an angiotensin-converting enzyme (ACE) inhibitor used to treat hypertension and heart failure. Enalapril is hydrolyzed in the liver to its active form, enalaprilat.

3. **Oseltamivir:** Oseltamivir phosphate is a prodrug of oseltamivir carboxylate, an antiviral medication used to treat influenza. Oseltamivir is converted to its active form by esterases in the body

Antimalarials

Introduction: Malaria, a life-threatening infectious disease transmitted through the bite of infected mosquitoes, remains a significant global health challenge, particularly in tropical and subtropical regions. Antimalarial drugs play a crucial role in the prevention and treatment of malaria, contributing to efforts to control and eliminate the disease. These medications target the Plasmodium parasites responsible for malaria, with different classes of antimalarials acting at various stages of the parasite's life cycle.

Types of Antimalarials:

1. **Artemisinin-Based Combination Therapies (ACTs):** ACTs are currently the most effective treatment for uncomplicated Plasmodium falciparum malaria, the most deadly malaria parasite species. Artemisinin, derived from the sweet wormwood plant (Artemisia annua), acts rapidly to reduce parasite load, while the partner drugs in ACTs (such as lumefantrine, piperaquine, or mefloquine) eliminate the remaining parasites. This combination therapy helps to prevent the development of drug resistance and improve treatment efficacy.

2. **Chloroquine and Hydroxychloroquine:** Once widely used for malaria prophylaxis and treatment, chloroquine and its derivative hydroxychloroquine are effective against susceptible strains of Plasmodium parasites.

However, widespread resistance has limited their utility in many regions. These drugs are still used for certain types of malaria and for autoimmune conditions like rheumatoid arthritis and lupus erythematosus.

3. **Quinoline Antimalarials:** Quinine, derived from the bark of the cinchona tree, was historically one of the earliest effective treatments for malaria. Its synthetic derivatives, including quinidine, mefloquine, and primaquine, are used for both treatment and prevention. These drugs act by disrupting the parasite's ability to digest hemoglobin, leading to its death.

4. **Antifolates:** Antifolate antimalarials, such as sulfadoxine-pyrimethamine (SP), inhibit the synthesis of folic acid, an essential nutrient for the parasite. These drugs are used in combination with other antimalarials for intermittent preventive treatment in pregnant women and infants, as well as for the treatment of uncomplicated malaria in areas with limited drug resistance.

Challenges and Considerations:

1. **Drug Resistance:** The emergence and spread of drug-resistant malaria parasites pose a significant challenge to malaria control efforts. Resistance to artemisinin, as well as partner drugs in ACTs, has been reported in certain regions, highlighting the need for continued surveillance and research into new treatment options.

2. **Side Effects:** Antimalarial drugs can cause various side effects, ranging from mild gastrointestinal disturbances to serious adverse reactions such as cardiotoxicity or neurotoxicity. Careful monitoring and appropriate dosing regimens are essential to minimize risks and

ensure patient safety.

3. **Access and Affordability:** Access to antimalarial drugs, particularly in resource-limited settings, remains a critical issue. Efforts to improve access, affordability, and distribution channels are essential for effective malaria control and elimination efforts.

Transmission Cycle

Malaria transmission occurs through the bite of infected female Anopheles mosquitoes, which serve as vectors for the Plasmodium parasites. When an infected mosquito bites a human host, it injects sporozoites—immature forms of the parasite—into the bloodstream. The sporozoites then travel to the liver, where they infect hepatocytes and undergo replication.

Within the liver cells, the parasites mature and multiply, eventually releasing merozoites into the bloodstream. These merozoites invade red blood cells (RBCs), where they continue to replicate asexually, causing the characteristic symptoms of malaria, including fever, chills, and anemia. Some parasites differentiate into sexual forms called gametocytes, which can be ingested by mosquitoes during a blood meal, completing the transmission cycle.

Factors Influencing Malaria Transmission: Several factors contribute to the complex dynamics of malaria transmission, including:

1. **Vector Biology:** The behavior, ecology, and susceptibility of Anopheles mosquitoes influence their capacity to transmit malaria. Factors such as mosquito species, population density, feeding habits, and breeding sites play a crucial role in determining transmission

intensity.

2. **Parasite Biology:** Variations in the biology, genetics, and virulence of Plasmodium parasites contribute to differences in disease severity and transmission dynamics. Certain parasite strains may exhibit resistance to antimalarial drugs or develop resistance to mosquito control measures.

3. **Environmental Factors:** Environmental conditions, including temperature, humidity, rainfall patterns, and land use, can influence mosquito breeding habitats, vector density, and malaria transmission dynamics. Climate change and human activities such as deforestation and urbanization can alter these factors, affecting malaria risk.

4. **Host Factors:** Human factors such as immunity, genetics, behavior, and socioeconomic status also influence malaria transmission and susceptibility to infection. Immunity acquired through previous exposure to malaria parasites can provide partial protection against severe disease, while certain genetic factors may confer resistance or susceptibility to infection.

Quinolines: Quinolines are a class of heterocyclic organic compounds characterized by a benzene ring fused to a pyridine ring. This unique chemical structure imbues quinolines with diverse pharmacological properties, making them valuable building blocks in drug discovery and development. From antimalarials to anticancer agents, quinolines have found application across various therapeutic areas, driving research into their synthesis, mechanism of action, and therapeutic potential.

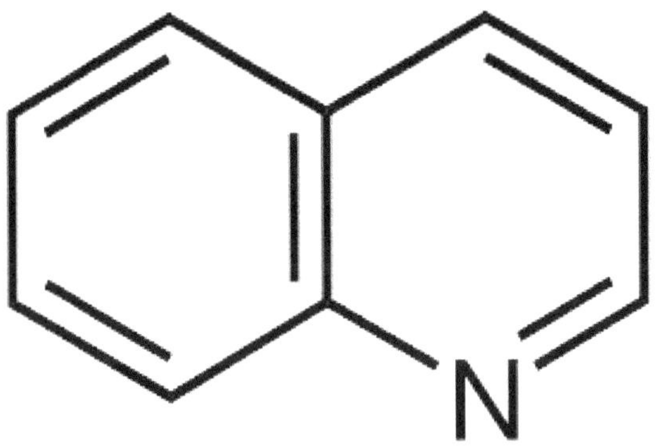

Chemical Structure and Synthesis: The basic structure of quinoline consists of a six-membered aromatic benzene ring fused to a five-membered pyridine ring. Quinolines can be synthesized through a variety of methods, including the Skraup synthesis, Doebner reaction, Friedländer synthesis, and Povarov reaction. These synthetic routes allow for the modification of quinoline derivatives to fine-tune their pharmacological properties and enhance their therapeutic efficacy.

Pharmacological Properties: Quinolines exhibit a wide range of pharmacological activities, including antimicrobial, antiviral, anticancer, anti-inflammatory, and central nervous system (CNS) effects. The diverse biological activities of quinolines stem from their ability to interact with various molecular targets within the body, including enzymes, receptors, and nucleic acids.

Therapeutic Applications:

1. **Antimalarials:** Quinoline-based antimalarial drugs, such as chloroquine and hydroxychloroquine, have been

instrumental in the treatment and prevention of malaria. These drugs exert their antimalarial effects by inhibiting the growth and replication of Plasmodium parasites within the host's red blood cells.

2. **Anticancer Agents:** Quinoline derivatives have shown promise as anticancer agents, with several compounds exhibiting cytotoxic activity against cancer cells. Compounds such as CQ1 and CQ2 have demonstrated selective toxicity towards cancer cells, making them potential candidates for further development as anticancer therapeutics.

3. **Antiviral Agents:** Quinolines have also been investigated for their antiviral properties, particularly against RNA viruses such as influenza and HIV. Compounds like T-705 (favipiravir) and remdesivir contain quinoline moieties and have shown efficacy against a range of viral infections.

4. **Anti-inflammatory Agents:** Certain quinoline derivatives possess anti-inflammatory activity and have been explored for the treatment of inflammatory conditions such as rheumatoid arthritis and inflammatory bowel disease. These compounds exert their effects by modulating inflammatory pathways and cytokine production.

5. **Central Nervous System (CNS) Agents:** Quinolines have shown potential as CNS agents, with some compounds exhibiting neuroprotective effects and others acting as ligands for neurotransmitter receptors. Compounds such as mefloquine have been investigated for their potential use in the treatment of neurodegenerative diseases like Alzheimer's and Parkinson's.

Quinine sulphate is a medication with a long and storied history in the treatment and prevention of malaria. Derived from the bark of the cinchona tree, quinine has been used for centuries by indigenous peoples of South America to treat fever and malaria. Today, while newer antimalarial drugs have largely replaced quinine as first-line treatment, it still holds a significant place in the therapeutic arsenal against malaria, particularly in cases of drug-resistant strains.

Chemical Properties and Synthesis: Quinine sulphate is an alkaloid compound with the chemical formula $C_{20}H_{24}N_2O_2 \cdot H_2SO_4$. It is a bitter-tasting, odorless crystalline substance that is sparingly soluble in water. Historically, quinine was extracted from the bark of various species of the cinchona tree. However, modern synthesis methods allow for the production of quinine sulphate through chemical processes involving the oxidation of quinoline derivatives.

Mechanism of Action: Quinine exerts its antimalarial effects primarily by interfering with the replication of Plasmodium parasites within the host's red blood cells. It acts by inhibiting the parasite's ability to digest hemoglobin, an essential nutrient for its survival. Additionally, quinine has been shown to disrupt the parasite's ability to polymerize hemoglobin, leading to the accumulation of toxic heme molecules and ultimately causing the death of the parasite.

Therapeutic Uses:

1. **Treatment of Malaria:** Quinine sulphate is primarily used in the treatment of uncomplicated and severe malaria caused by Plasmodium falciparum, particularly in regions where drug resistance is prevalent. It is often

used in combination with other antimalarial drugs to enhance efficacy and reduce the risk of resistance development.

2. **Prevention of Malaria:** While quinine is less commonly used for malaria prevention (chemoprophylaxis) due to its side effects and the availability of other drugs with better tolerability profiles, it may still be prescribed in certain situations, such as for travelers to areas with chloroquine-resistant malaria.

Chloroquine is a medication with a multifaceted history, originally developed as an antimalarial drug and subsequently found to have broader therapeutic applications. While its use as a first-line treatment for malaria has declined due to emerging resistance, chloroquine remains relevant in the management of certain infections and autoimmune diseases. Additionally, ongoing research continues to uncover new potential uses for this versatile compound.

Chemical Structure and Mechanism of Action: Chloroquine is a 4-aminoquinoline compound with the chemical formula $C_{18}H_{26}C_lN_3$. It acts primarily by accumulating within the acidic environment of the parasite's food vacuole, disrupting its ability to detoxify and metabolize heme, resulting in the accumulation of toxic heme aggregates and subsequent death of the parasite. This mechanism of action makes chloroquine effective against various species of Plasmodium parasites responsible for malaria.

Therapeutic Uses:

1. **Malaria Treatment and Prophylaxis:** Chloroquine was

historically one of the most widely used antimalarial drugs due to its efficacy, low cost, and relative safety. It was used for both the treatment and prevention of malaria, particularly in regions where Plasmodium falciparum, the most deadly malaria parasite species, was susceptible. However, widespread resistance to chloroquine has significantly reduced its effectiveness in many areas, leading to its replacement by other antimalarial drugs.

2. **Autoimmune Diseases:** Chloroquine and its derivative hydroxychloroquine have been used in the treatment of autoimmune diseases such as rheumatoid arthritis, systemic lupus erythematosus (SLE), and certain dermatological conditions. These drugs exhibit immunomodulatory effects, including inhibition of inflammatory cytokines and interference with antigen presentation, leading to their utility in managing autoimmune-related inflammation and symptoms.

3. **Antiviral Activity:** Chloroquine has garnered attention for its potential antiviral properties, particularly against certain RNA viruses such as coronaviruses. Studies have suggested that chloroquine may inhibit viral replication by interfering with viral entry, endosomal acidification, and glycosylation of cellular receptors. While its efficacy against specific viral infections remains under investigation, chloroquine has been explored as a potential treatment for emerging infectious diseases such as COVID-19.

Side Effects and Precautions: While chloroquine is generally well-tolerated, it can cause various side effects, including gastrointestinal disturbances, headache, blurred vision, and skin reactions. Prolonged use or high doses may lead to more serious adverse effects, such as retinopathy, cardiotoxicity, and neuromyopathy. Therefore, chloroquine should be used cautiously and under medical supervision, particularly in patients with pre-existing conditions or risk factors for toxicity.

Amodiaquine

Introduction: Amodiaquine is an antimalarial medication that has been used for decades in the treatment and prevention of malaria, particularly in regions where resistance to other antimalarials is prevalent. Although its use declined due to concerns about safety and tolerability, amodiaquine has experienced a resurgence of interest in recent years, driven by its effectiveness against certain drug-resistant strains of malaria parasites.

Chemical Structure and Mechanism of Action: Amodiaquine belongs to the 4-aminoquinoline class of antimalarial drugs, sharing structural similarities with chloroquine. Its chemical formula is $C_{20}H_{22}C_lN_3O$. Similar to chloroquine, amodiaquine exerts its antimalarial effects by accumulating within the acidic environment of the parasite's food vacuole, interfering with heme metabolism, and ultimately leading to parasite death. However, it also exhibits some differences in its pharmacokinetic and pharmacodynamic properties compared to chloroquine.

Therapeutic Uses:

1. **Malaria Treatment:** Amodiaquine is primarily used in the treatment of uncomplicated malaria caused by Plasmodium falciparum, particularly in regions where resistance to other antimalarial drugs is prevalent. It is often used in combination with other antimalarials, such as artesunate, to improve treatment efficacy and

reduce the risk of resistance development. Amodiaquine-based combination therapies (ACTs) have been recommended by the World Health Organization (WHO) as a first-line treatment for malaria in certain regions.

2. **Malaria Prophylaxis:** While not commonly used for malaria prevention (chemoprophylaxis) due to safety concerns and the availability of other drugs with better tolerability profiles, amodiaquine may be prescribed in certain situations, such as for travelers to areas with multidrug-resistant malaria parasites.

Side Effects and Precautions: Amodiaquine is generally well-tolerated, but like other antimalarial drugs, it can cause side effects, including gastrointestinal disturbances, headache, dizziness, and itching. Rare but serious adverse reactions, such as hepatotoxicity, hematologic disorders, and skin reactions, can occur, particularly with prolonged use or high doses. Amodiaquine should be used with caution and under medical supervision, especially in patients with pre-existing liver or kidney conditions.

Primaquine phosphate is an essential medication in the treatment and prevention of malaria, particularly in regions where Plasmodium vivax or Plasmodium ovale malaria is prevalent. Its distinct mechanism of action and ability to target hypnozoites—a dormant form of the malaria parasite—make it indispensable in the effort to control and eliminate malaria.

Chemical Structure and Mechanism of Action: Primaquine phosphate is a synthetic derivative of the natural compound quinoline. Its chemical formula is $C_{15}H_{21}N_3O$. Primaquine works by disrupting the life cycle of the malaria parasite, targeting both the replicating form (schizonts) and the dormant liver stage (hypnozoites). While its precise mechanism of action is not fully understood, primaquine is believed to interfere with the metabolism of heme, leading to the accumulation of toxic byproducts and eventual death of the parasite.

Therapeutic Uses:

1. **Treatment of Vivax and Ovale Malaria:** Primaquine phosphate is primarily used in the treatment of malaria caused by Plasmodium vivax or Plasmodium ovale. Unlike other antimalarial drugs that target the blood stage of the parasite, primaquine is uniquely effective against the dormant hypnozoite stage, which can persist in the liver and cause relapses months or even years after the initial infection. By eliminating hypnozoites, primaquine prevents relapses and contributes to complete cure.
2. **Malaria Prophylaxis:** Primaquine is also used for malaria prophylaxis (prevention) in certain circumstances, particularly in individuals traveling to areas where Plasmodium vivax or Plasmodium ovale malaria is prevalent. Its ability to target the liver stage of the parasite makes it effective in preventing relapses following exposure to malaria.

Side Effects and Precautions: While primaquine phosphate is generally safe and well-tolerated, it can cause side effects in some individuals. Common side effects may include gastrointestinal disturbances (such as nausea, vomiting, and abdominal pain), headache, and dizziness. Rare but serious adverse reactions, such as hemolytic anemia in individuals with glucose-6-phosphate dehydrogenase (G6PD) deficiency, may occur and require careful screening before initiating treatment.

Pamaquine:

Introduction: Pamaquine, also known as plasmochin or plasmoquine, is an antimalarial medication with a long history of use in the prevention and treatment of malaria. While not as commonly prescribed today as some other antimalarial drugs, pamaquine still holds significance in certain contexts, particularly in regions where specific strains of malaria parasites are prevalent.

Mechanism of Action: Pamaquine belongs to the class of medications known as 8-aminoquinolines, similar to primaquine. Its mechanism of action involves interfering with the metabolism of the malaria parasite, particularly targeting the forms of the parasite that reside in the liver (hypnozoites) and those circulating in the blood. By disrupting the parasite's lifecycle, pamaquine helps to eradicate the malaria infection from the body.

Uses:

1. **Malaria Treatment:** Pamaquine has historically been used in the treatment of malaria caused by various Plasmodium species, including Plasmodium vivax and Plasmodium ovale. It is particularly effective against the liver stages of the malaria parasite, making it useful in eliminating dormant forms of the parasite that may lead to relapse.

2. **Malaria Prophylaxis:** While not commonly used for malaria prevention today, pamaquine has been employed as a prophylactic medication for individuals traveling to regions where malaria is endemic. However, due to concerns about side effects and the availability of

other antimalarial drugs with better safety profiles, its use for prophylaxis has diminished over time.

Dosage: The dosage of pamaquine varies depending on factors such as the patient's age, weight, and the specific strain of malaria being treated. It is typically administered orally, and the dosage regimen may differ for treatment and prophylaxis. Dosage adjustments may be necessary for patients with liver or kidney impairment. As with any medication, it's crucial to follow the prescribed dosage and regimen provided by a healthcare professional.

Side Effects: Pamaquine, like other antimalarial medications, can cause side effects in some individuals. Common side effects may include nausea, vomiting, abdominal pain, headache, and dizziness. In some cases, pamaquine may also cause more serious adverse reactions, such as hemolytic anemia, particularly in individuals with glucose-6-phosphate dehydrogenase (G6PD) deficiency. Patients should be monitored for any signs of adverse reactions, and medical attention should be sought if any concerning symptoms arise.

Precautions: Before initiating treatment with pamaquine, patients should inform their healthcare provider about any pre-existing medical conditions, allergies, or medications they are currently taking. Special caution is advised for individuals with G6PD deficiency, as pamaquine can cause hemolysis in these individuals. Pregnant and breastfeeding women should also exercise caution and consult with a healthcare professional before taking pamaquine.

Quinacrine hydrochloride :- also known by its trade name Atabrine or mepacrine, is a medication with a rich history in the treatment and prevention of malaria. Beyond its antimalarial properties, quinacrine hydrochloride has also been utilized for its antiprotozoal activity in various medical applications.

Mechanism of Action: Quinacrine hydrochloride exerts its pharmacological effects by interfering with the growth and reproduction of malaria parasites. It primarily targets the asexual erythrocytic forms of the parasite, preventing their ability to proliferate within the human host. Additionally, quinacrine hydrochloride exhibits activity against other protozoal parasites, such as those causing giardiasis and amoebiasis.

Uses:

Malaria Treatment: Quinacrine hydrochloride was one of the earliest synthetic antimalarial drugs to be developed and widely used. It has been employed in the treatment of various forms of malaria, including uncomplicated and severe cases caused by Plasmodium falciparum, Plasmodium vivax, Plasmodium malariae, and Plasmodium ovale. However, its use as a first-line treatment for malaria has declined over time due to the availability of newer and more effective antimalarial medications with better safety profiles.

Malaria Prophylaxis: Quinacrine hydrochloride has been used for malaria prophylaxis in individuals traveling to regions where malaria is endemic. However, similar to its therapeutic use, its role in prophylaxis has diminished due to concerns about side effects and the availability of alternative medications with fewer adverse reactions.

Antiprotozoal Therapy: In addition to its antimalarial properties, quinacrine hydrochloride is effective against other protozoal parasites. It has been used in the treatment of giardiasis, a common intestinal infection caused by the parasite Giardia lamblia, as well as in the management of certain cases of amoebiasis, caused by the parasite Entamoeba histolytica.

Dosage: The dosage of quinacrine hydrochloride varies depending on the specific condition being treated, as well as factors such as the patient's age, weight, and medical history. It is typically administered orally in tablet or capsule form. Dosage adjustments may be necessary for patients with liver or kidney impairment. As with any medication, it's essential to follow the prescribed dosage and regimen provided by a healthcare professional.

Side Effects: Quinacrine hydrochloride can cause side effects in some individuals. Common side effects may include gastrointestinal disturbances such as nausea, vomiting, and diarrhea, as well as headache, dizziness, and skin reactions. Long-term use or high doses of quinacrine hydrochloride may result in more serious adverse effects, including ocular toxicity and neuropsychiatric symptoms. Patients should be monitored for any signs of adverse reactions, and medical attention should be sought if any concerning symptoms arise.

Precautions: Before initiating treatment with quinacrine hydrochloride, patients should inform their healthcare provider about any pre-existing medical conditions, allergies, or medications they are currently taking. Special caution is advised for pregnant and breastfeeding women, as well as individuals with liver or kidney impairment. Quinacrine hydrochloride should be used with caution in patients with a history of psychiatric disorders or epilepsy. Additionally, regular ophthalmic examinations may be recommended for patients receiving long-term treatment with quinacrine hydrochloride to monitor for ocular toxicity.

Mefloquine :- marketed under the trade name Lariam among others, is an important antimalarial medication known for its efficacy in preventing and treating malaria. It belongs to the class of medications called antimalarials and is particularly effective against malaria caused by Plasmodium falciparum, including drug-resistant strains. Mefloquine is often used for malaria prophylaxis in travelers visiting regions where the disease is endemic and as a treatment for acute malaria infections.

Mechanism of Action: Mefloquine exerts its antimalarial effects by interfering with the parasite's ability to metabolize and utilize hemoglobin, essential for its survival within the red blood cells. It primarily targets the asexual blood stages of the malaria parasite, inhibiting its growth and replication. Additionally, mefloquine may also have activity against the liver stages of the parasite, helping to prevent relapses in certain types of malaria.

Uses:

Malaria Prophylaxis: Mefloquine is widely used for malaria prophylaxis in travelers visiting regions where malaria transmission is prevalent, particularly in areas with chloroquine-resistant Plasmodium falciparum. It is typically taken weekly starting one to two weeks before entering the malaria-endemic area, continued throughout the stay, and continued for four weeks after leaving the area.

Malaria Treatment: Mefloquine is also used in the treatment of acute malaria infections, particularly those caused by Plasmodium falciparum. It may be used alone or in combination with other antimalarial medications, depending on the severity of the infection and local drug resistance patterns. However, it is not recommended for severe malaria cases.

Dosage: The dosage of mefloquine for prophylaxis and treatment varies depending on factors such as the patient's age, weight, and the specific condition being treated. For malaria prophylaxis, the typical adult dosage is 250 mg once weekly, while for treatment, the dosage may range from 750 mg as a single dose to 1250 mg over a three-day period. It is important to follow the prescribed dosage and regimen provided by a healthcare professional to ensure the medication's effectiveness and minimize the risk of adverse effects.

Side Effects: While mefloquine is generally well-tolerated, it can cause side effects in some individuals. Common side effects may include nausea, vomiting, diarrhea, dizziness, headache, and sleep disturbances. More serious adverse reactions such as psychiatric symptoms (including anxiety, depression, and hallucinations), seizures, and cardiac effects (including QT interval prolongation) have been reported, albeit rarely. Patients should be monitored for any signs of adverse reactions, and medical attention should be sought if any concerning symptoms arise.

Precautions: Before initiating treatment with mefloquine, patients should inform their healthcare provider about any pre-existing medical conditions, allergies, or medications they are currently taking. Mefloquine should be used with caution in individuals with a history of psychiatric disorders, seizures, cardiac arrhythmias, or liver impairment. Pregnant and breastfeeding women should also consult with a healthcare professional before taking mefloquine, as its safety during pregnancy and lactation has not been fully established.

Cycloguanil pamoate :- is a pharmaceutical compound used primarily in the treatment and prevention of malaria. It is a prodrug, meaning it undergoes chemical conversion within the body to its active form, cycloguanil, which exerts its antimalarial effects. Cycloguanil pamoate is often used in combination with other antimalarial medications to enhance efficacy and reduce the risk of drug resistance.

Mechanism of Action: Cycloguanil, the active metabolite of cycloguanil pamoate, inhibits the dihydrofolate reductase enzyme in the malaria parasite Plasmodium falciparum. By disrupting the parasite's ability to synthesize essential folate cofactors, cycloguanil prevents the production of DNA and RNA, ultimately leading to the death of the parasite. This mechanism of action is similar to that of other antimalarial drugs such as pyrimethamine.

Uses:

Malaria Treatment: Cycloguanil pamoate is primarily used in the treatment of malaria caused by Plasmodium falciparum, particularly in combination with other antimalarial medications such as sulfadoxine. The combination therapy of cycloguanil and sulfadoxine, known as sulfadoxine-pyrimethamine (SP) or Fansidar, has been used extensively in the past for the treatment of uncomplicated malaria. However, due to the emergence of drug-resistant strains of malaria, its use has become limited in some regions.

Malaria Prophylaxis: While less commonly used for malaria prophylaxis compared to other antimalarial medications, cycloguanil pamoate has been investigated for its potential role in preventing malaria in travelers visiting endemic regions. Its use in prophylaxis may be considered in certain situations, particularly when other prophylactic options are not available or suitable.

Dosage: The dosage of cycloguanil pamoate varies depending on factors such as the patient's age, weight, and the specific condition being treated. It is typically administered orally in tablet or suspension form. The recommended dosage regimen may differ for malaria treatment and prophylaxis. Patients should follow the prescribed dosage and regimen provided by a healthcare professional to ensure the medication's effectiveness and minimize the risk of adverse effects.

Side Effects: Cycloguanil pamoate can cause side effects in some individuals. Common side effects may include gastrointestinal disturbances such as nausea, vomiting, and diarrhea, as well as headache, dizziness, and allergic reactions. In rare cases, cycloguanil pamoate may cause more serious adverse reactions such as hematologic disorders (e.g., agranulocytosis, aplastic anemia) or hepatic toxicity. Patients should be monitored for any signs of adverse reactions, and medical attention should be sought if any concerning symptoms arise.

Precautions: Before initiating treatment with cycloguanil pamoate, patients should inform their healthcare provider about any pre-existing medical conditions, allergies, or medications they are currently taking. Special caution is advised for pregnant and breastfeeding women, as well as individuals with liver or kidney impairment. Cycloguanil pamoate should be used with caution in patients with a history of hematologic disorders or hypersensitivity reactions to other antimalarial medications.

Proguanil :- often marketed under the brand name Paludrine, is a widely recognized antimalarial medication used for both treatment and prophylaxis against malaria. It belongs to the class of medications known as antifolates and is particularly effective against Plasmodium falciparum and Plasmodium vivax malaria. Proguanil is commonly used in combination with other antimalarial drugs to enhance efficacy and reduce the risk of drug resistance.

Mechanism of Action: Proguanil undergoes metabolic conversion within the body to its active form, cycloguanil, which acts as a competitive inhibitor of the dihydrofolate reductase enzyme in the malaria parasite Plasmodium falciparum. By disrupting folate metabolism, cycloguanil inhibits the synthesis of DNA and RNA, ultimately leading to the death of the parasite. This mechanism of action is similar to that of other antifolate antimalarial drugs such as pyrimethamine.

Uses:

Malaria Prophylaxis: Proguanil is commonly used for malaria prophylaxis in travelers visiting regions where malaria transmission is prevalent. It is often used in combination with other antimalarial medications such as atovaquone (as in Malarone) or chloroquine (as in Paludrine/Avloclor) for enhanced efficacy. Proguanil is typically initiated one to two days before travel, continued throughout the stay in the malaria-endemic area, and continued for four weeks after leaving the area.

Malaria Treatment: Proguanil is also used in the treatment of malaria, particularly in combination therapy regimens. When combined with other antimalarial medications such as chloroquine or artesunate, proguanil can effectively treat uncomplicated malaria caused by susceptible strains of Plasmodium falciparum and Plasmodium vivax. However, it may not be effective against certain drug-resistant strains of malaria.

Dosage: The dosage of proguanil varies depending on factors such as the patient's age, weight, and the specific condition being treated. For malaria prophylaxis, the typical adult dosage is 200 mg (one tablet) once daily, while for treatment, the dosage may vary depending on the specific combination therapy regimen being used. Patients should follow the prescribed dosage and regimen provided by a healthcare professional to ensure the medication's effectiveness and minimize the risk of adverse effects.

Side Effects: Proguanil is generally well-tolerated, but like all medications, it can cause side effects in some individuals. Common side effects may include gastrointestinal disturbances such as nausea, vomiting, and diarrhea, as well as headache, dizziness, and mouth ulcers. In rare cases, proguanil may cause more serious adverse reactions such as hematologic disorders (e.g., leukopenia, thrombocytopenia) or hypersensitivity reactions. Patients should be monitored for any signs of adverse reactions, and medical attention should be sought if any concerning symptoms arise.

Precautions: Before initiating treatment with proguanil, patients should inform their healthcare provider about any pre-existing medical conditions, allergies, or medications they are currently taking. Proguanil should be used with caution in patients with liver or kidney impairment, as dosage adjustments may be necessary. Pregnant and breastfeeding women should also consult with a healthcare professional before taking proguanil, as its safety during pregnancy and lactation has not been fully established.

Pyrimethamine :- also known by its trade name Daraprim, is a medication primarily used in the prevention and treatment of malaria. This pharmaceutical compound belongs to the class of medications called antiprotozoals. Its mechanism of action involves inhibiting the enzyme dihydrofolate reductase, which is essential for the synthesis of nucleic acids in certain organisms, including the malaria parasite Plasmodium falciparum.

History and Development

Pyrimethamine was first synthesized in the 1950s by American scientist and Nobel laureate Gertrude B. Elion, along with her colleagues George Hitchings and Sir James Black. Their groundbreaking work in drug development revolutionized the treatment of various diseases, including malaria.

Medical Uses

1. **Malaria Treatment**: Pyrimethamine is highly effective against malaria caused by Plasmodium falciparum, particularly in combination with other antimalarial drugs such as sulfadoxine. It works by disrupting the growth and reproduction of the parasite within the red blood cells, thereby helping to clear the infection.
2. **Toxoplasmosis**: Pyrimethamine is also used in the treatment and prevention of toxoplasmosis, a parasitic infection caused by Toxoplasma gondii. This condition can be particularly dangerous for individuals with weakened immune systems, such as those living with HIV/AIDS or undergoing organ transplantation.

Dosage and Administration

Pyrimethamine is typically administered orally in the form of tablets. The dosage and duration of treatment may vary depending on the patient's age, weight, medical condition, and the severity of the infection. It is often prescribed in combination with other medications, such as sulfadoxine or sulfadiazine, to enhance its efficacy and reduce the risk of drug resistance.

Side Effects

While pyrimethamine is generally well-tolerated, like any medication, it may cause side effects in some individuals. Common side effects may include:

- Nausea
- Vomiting
- Diarrhea
- Headache
- Dizziness
- Rash
- Allergic reactions

In rare cases, pyrimethamine may cause more serious side effects, such as bone marrow suppression or liver toxicity. Patients should seek medical attention if they experience any severe or persistent adverse reactions while taking this medication.

Precautions and Warnings

- Pyrimethamine should be used with caution in individuals with a history of folate deficiency or megaloblastic anemia, as it may exacerbate these conditions.
- Pregnant women should consult with their healthcare provider before taking pyrimethamine, as it may pose risks to the developing fetus, particularly during the first trimester.
- Pyrimethamine may interact with other medications, including anticonvulsants, antifolate drugs, and certain

antibiotics. Patients should inform their healthcare provider about all the medications they are taking to avoid potential drug interactions.

Artesunate is a key player in the battle against malaria, a disease that continues to pose a significant global health challenge, particularly in tropical and subtropical regions. This medication belongs to the class of drugs known as artemisinin derivatives, which are derived from the sweet wormwood plant (Artemisia annua). Artesunate is renowned for its potent antimalarial properties and is widely used as a first-line treatment for uncomplicated malaria caused by Plasmodium falciparum, the deadliest species of malaria parasite.

History and Development

The discovery of artemisinin, the parent compound from which derivatives like artesunate are derived, is credited to Chinese scientist Tu Youyou, who was awarded the Nobel Prize in Physiology or Medicine in 2015 for her groundbreaking work. Artemisinin-based combination therapies (ACTs), which combine artemisinin derivatives with other antimalarial drugs, have since become the cornerstone of malaria treatment and prevention efforts worldwide, owing to their high efficacy and rapid action against the malaria parasite.

Mechanism of Action

Artesunate exerts its antimalarial effects by a mechanism that involves the generation of free radicals within the malaria parasite, leading to damage to its cell membranes and other vital structures. This mode of action results in the rapid clearance of parasitic infections from the bloodstream, helping to alleviate symptoms and prevent the progression of severe malaria, which can be life-threatening if left untreated.

Medical Uses

Artesunate is primarily used for the treatment of uncomplicated malaria, particularly in regions where Plasmodium falciparum is prevalent and resistance to other antimalarial drugs is a concern. It is available in various formulations, including oral tablets, injectable solutions, and rectal suppositories, allowing for flexible administration based on the patient's age, condition, and accessibility to healthcare facilities.

Dosage and Administration

The dosage and administration of artesunate may vary depending on factors such as the severity of the malaria infection, the patient's age and weight, and the formulation of the medication. In general, oral artesunate is administered in combination with other antimalarial drugs as part of an ACT regimen, typically over a course of three days. Injectable artesunate may be used in cases of severe malaria or when oral administration is not feasible.

Safety and Side Effects

Artesunate is generally well-tolerated, with few reported adverse effects. Common side effects may include:

- Nausea
- Vomiting
- Diarrhea
- Dizziness
- Headache
- Allergic reactions (rare)

Serious side effects are rare but may include severe allergic reactions, hemolysis (breakdown of red blood cells), and neurological effects. Patients should seek medical attention if they experience any unusual symptoms or adverse reactions while taking artesunate.

Artemether is a vital component in the arsenal against malaria, a disease that disproportionately affects tropical and subtropical regions, particularly in Africa. This medication belongs to the class of drugs known as artemisinin derivatives, derived from the sweet wormwood plant (Artemisia annua). Artemether, along with its sister compound artesunate, plays a crucial role in the treatment of malaria, particularly infections caused by the deadliest malaria parasite, Plasmodium falciparum.

Discovery and Development

The discovery of artemisinin, the parent compound from which derivatives like artemether are derived, is attributed to Chinese scientist Tu Youyou, who received the Nobel Prize in Physiology or Medicine in 2015 for her pioneering work. Artemisinin-based combination therapies (ACTs), which combine artemisinin derivatives with other antimalarial drugs, have since become the cornerstone of malaria treatment due to their high efficacy and rapid action against the malaria parasite.

Mechanism of Action

Artemether exerts its antimalarial effects through a mechanism similar to other artemisinin derivatives. It triggers the release of free radicals within the malaria parasite, leading to damage to its cell membranes and other vital structures. This mode of action results in the rapid clearance of parasitic infections from the bloodstream, alleviating symptoms and preventing the progression of severe malaria.

Medical Uses

Artemether is primarily used in the treatment of uncomplicated malaria caused by Plasmodium falciparum. It is often administered in combination with other antimalarial drugs, such as lumefantrine, to enhance its efficacy and reduce the risk of drug resistance. Artemether-based combination therapies (ACTs) are recommended by the World Health Organization (WHO) as first-line treatments for malaria in regions where Plasmodium falciparum is prevalent.

Dosage and Administration

The dosage and administration of artemether may vary depending on factors such as the severity of the malaria infection, the patient's age and weight, and the formulation of the medication. Artemether-lumefantrine combination therapy is typically administered orally over a course of three days. In cases of severe malaria or when oral administration is not feasible, injectable formulations of artemether may be used.

Safety and Side Effects

Artemether is generally well-tolerated, with few reported adverse effects. Common side effects may include:

- Nausea
- Vomiting
- Diarrhea
- Dizziness
- Headache
- Allergic reactions (rare)

Serious side effects are uncommon but may include severe allergic reactions, hemolysis (breakdown of red blood cells), and neurological effects. Patients should seek medical attention if they experience any unusual symptoms or adverse reactions while taking artemether.

Atovaquone was initially developed in the late 1980s by scientists at GlaxoSmithKline (GSK) in collaboration with academic researchers. Its development was driven by the urgent need for new and effective antimalarial drugs, particularly in the face of increasing resistance to existing therapies. Since its introduction, atovaquone has become an essential component of combination therapies for malaria and has demonstrated efficacy against various other parasitic infections.

Mechanism of Action

The mechanism of action of atovaquone differs from that of traditional antimalarial drugs like chloroquine or artemisinin derivatives. Atovaquone targets the mitochondrial electron transport chain of the parasite, disrupting its energy production and ultimately leading to its death. This unique mode of action makes atovaquone effective against a broad spectrum of protozoal pathogens, including Plasmodium species responsible for malaria, as well as Toxoplasma gondii and Pneumocystis jirovecii, among others.

Medical Uses

1. **Malaria Treatment and Prevention**: Atovaquone is widely used in combination with proguanil (sold under the trade name Malarone) for the treatment and prevention of malaria caused by Plasmodium falciparum and Plasmodium vivax. Malarone has become a popular choice for travelers to malaria-endemic regions due to its efficacy, tolerability, and convenient dosing regimen.
2. **Toxoplasmosis**: Atovaquone is also employed in the treatment of toxoplasmosis, a parasitic infection caused

by Toxoplasma gondii. This condition can be particularly severe in individuals with compromised immune systems, such as those living with HIV/AIDS or undergoing organ transplantation.

3. **Pneumocystis Pneumonia**: Atovaquone is used as an alternative treatment for Pneumocystis pneumonia (PCP) in patients who cannot tolerate or do not respond to standard therapy with trimethoprim-sulfamethoxazole (TMP-SMX), the first-line treatment for PCP.

Dosage and Administration

Atovaquone is typically administered orally in the form of tablets or suspension. The dosage and duration of treatment may vary depending on the specific indication, the patient's age, weight, and medical history. For malaria prevention, atovaquone-proguanil combination tablets are usually taken once daily, starting one or two days before entering a malaria-endemic area and continuing throughout the stay and for a week after leaving the area.

Side Effects

Atovaquone is generally well-tolerated, with few reported side effects. Common side effects may include:

- Nausea
- Vomiting
- Diarrhea
- Abdominal pain
- Headache
- Rash

Serious adverse reactions are rare but may include liver toxicity and allergic reactions. Patients should seek medical attention if they experience any severe or persistent side effects while taking atovaquone.

Anti-tubercular Agents

Tuberculosis (TB) remains one of the world's deadliest infectious diseases, claiming millions of lives each year. The battle against TB is waged on multiple fronts, with prevention, diagnosis, and treatment being key pillars in the fight against this ancient disease. Central to the treatment of TB are anti-tubercular agents, a diverse array of medications designed to combat the causative agent of TB, Mycobacterium tuberculosis.

Overview of Tuberculosis Treatment

Tuberculosis treatment typically involves a combination of several drugs administered over a prolonged period. This approach, known as directly observed therapy short-course (DOTS), aims to ensure effective treatment, prevent the emergence of drug resistance, and reduce the risk of relapse. The World Health Organization (WHO) recommends a standard regimen for the treatment of drug-susceptible TB, consisting of four first-line drugs:

1. **Isoniazid (INH):** Isoniazid is a cornerstone of TB treatment, exerting its antimycobacterial effects by inhibiting the synthesis of mycolic acids, essential components of the mycobacterial cell wall. It is highly effective against actively dividing and dormant bacilli.

2. **Rifampicin (RIF):** Rifampicin is another key component of TB therapy, acting by inhibiting bacterial RNA synthesis. Its potent bactericidal activity makes it essential for the eradication of TB bacteria.

3. **Pyrazinamide (PZA):** Pyrazinamide is particularly active against Mycobacterium tuberculosis residing in

acidic environments, such as within macrophages. It plays a crucial role in shortening the duration of TB treatment.

4. **Ethambutol (EMB)**: Ethambutol disrupts mycobacterial cell wall synthesis by inhibiting the formation of arabinogalactan, a critical component of the cell envelope. It is often used in combination with other first-line drugs to prevent the emergence of drug resistance.

In addition to these first-line drugs, second-line agents are employed in the treatment of drug-resistant TB. These medications include fluoroquinolones, injectable agents (such as kanamycin, amikacin, and capreomycin), and newer drugs like bedaquiline and delamanid. Treatment regimens for drug-resistant TB are more complex and may require prolonged therapy with multiple drugs, often accompanied by close monitoring for adverse effects and drug interactions.

Challenges and Advances

Despite the availability of effective anti-tubercular agents, tuberculosis treatment still faces significant challenges. These include the emergence of drug-resistant strains, particularly multidrug-resistant TB (MDR-TB) and extensively drug-resistant TB (XDR-TB), as well as issues related to treatment adherence, access to care, and the complexity of treatment regimens.

To address these challenges, ongoing research efforts focus on the development of new TB drugs with novel mechanisms of action, improved efficacy, and reduced toxicity. Additionally, strategies to optimize treatment regimens, enhance treatment adherence, and strengthen healthcare systems are critical components of global TB control efforts.

Isoniazid :- often abbreviated as INH, stands as a cornerstone in the treatment of tuberculosis (TB), a disease caused by the bacterium Mycobacterium tuberculosis. Since its introduction in the 1950s, isoniazid has played a pivotal role in reducing TB-related morbidity and mortality worldwide. This medication is a first-line drug for the treatment of both latent TB infection and active TB disease, forming an integral part of standard anti-tubercular regimens.

Mechanism of Action

The effectiveness of isoniazid against TB stems from its ability to inhibit the synthesis of mycolic acids, essential components of the mycobacterial cell wall. By targeting the enzyme enoyl-ACP reductase (InhA), which is involved in the synthesis of fatty acids, isoniazid disrupts the integrity of the mycobacterial cell envelope. This interference with cell wall synthesis ultimately leads to the death of the TB bacteria.

Medical Uses

1. **Treatment of Active Tuberculosis**: Isoniazid is a key component of the standard short-course treatment regimen for active TB disease. Administered orally either alone or in combination with other first-line anti-tubercular agents (such as rifampicin, pyrazinamide, and ethambutol), isoniazid is highly effective in killing the bacteria responsible for TB.

2. **Prevention of Latent Tuberculosis Infection**: Isoniazid is also utilized for the prevention of latent TB infection from progressing to active TB disease. Known as latent TB therapy or prophylaxis, this treatment approach involves administering isoniazid to individuals who have been exposed to TB but do not have active disease. By eliminating latent TB bacteria, isoniazid helps prevent the development of active TB and reduces the risk of transmission to others.

Dosage and Administration

Isoniazid is typically administered orally as a tablet or syrup. The dosage and duration of treatment vary depending on the patient's age, weight, medical history, and the specific indication for which it is being used. In the treatment of active TB, isoniazid is usually taken once daily, often as part of a combination regimen, for a duration of six to nine months. For latent TB therapy, isoniazid may be taken daily for six to nine months, although shorter regimens (e.g., three months of daily isoniazid and rifapentine) are also recommended in certain situations.

Side Effects

While isoniazid is generally well-tolerated, it may cause side effects in some individuals. Common side effects may include:

- Nausea
- Vomiting
- Abdominal pain
- Peripheral neuropathy (numbness, tingling, or weakness in the extremities)
- Hepatotoxicity (liver damage)

Rare but serious side effects may include severe allergic reactions, hepatitis, and hematologic abnormalities. Patients should be monitored closely for signs of adverse reactions while taking isoniazid, and healthcare providers should be notified if any concerning symptoms develop.

Ethionamide is a medication widely used in the treatment of tuberculosis (TB), particularly in cases of drug-resistant TB where standard first-line medications are ineffective. As a member of the second-line anti-tubercular drugs, ethionamide plays a crucial role in combating drug-resistant strains of Mycobacterium tuberculosis, the bacterium responsible for TB.

Mechanism of Action

Ethionamide exerts its antimycobacterial effects by inhibiting the synthesis of mycolic acids, key components of the mycobacterial cell wall. Similar to isoniazid, ethionamide targets the enzyme enoyl-ACP reductase (InhA), disrupting fatty acid synthesis in the TB bacteria. This disruption leads to cell wall damage and ultimately bacterial death.

Medical Uses

1. **Treatment of Drug-Resistant Tuberculosis:** Ethionamide is a vital component of the treatment regimen for drug-resistant TB, including multidrug-resistant TB (MDR-TB) and extensively drug-resistant

TB (XDR-TB). In combination with other second-line drugs, such as fluoroquinolones and injectable agents, ethionamide helps to eradicate drug-resistant TB bacteria and prevent disease progression.

2. **Adjuvant Therapy for Drug-Susceptible Tuberculosis**: In some cases of drug-susceptible TB, ethionamide may be used as an adjuvant therapy when first-line medications are contraindicated or ineffective. It may be included in treatment regimens for patients with comorbidities, drug allergies, or intolerance to standard anti-tubercular drugs.

Dosage and Administration

Ethionamide is typically administered orally in the form of tablets. The dosage and duration of treatment vary depending on factors such as the severity of the TB infection, the patient's weight, and the presence of drug resistance. Ethionamide is often prescribed in combination with other second-line anti-tubercular drugs, and treatment regimens may be tailored based on drug susceptibility testing and individual patient factors.

Side Effects

While ethionamide is generally well-tolerated, it may cause side effects in some individuals. Common side effects may include:

- Gastrointestinal disturbances (nausea, vomiting, diarrhea)
- Abdominal pain
- Metallic taste
- Central nervous system effects (dizziness, headache, confusion)

- Hepatotoxicity (liver damage)

Rare but serious side effects may include peripheral neuropathy, hypothyroidism, and hematologic abnormalities. Patients should be monitored closely for signs of adverse reactions while taking ethionamide, and healthcare providers should be notified if any concerning symptoms develop.

Ethambutol :- is a key medication in the treatment of tuberculosis (TB), a bacterial infection caused by Mycobacterium tuberculosis. Since its introduction, ethambutol has been an essential component of standard anti-tubercular regimens, particularly in combination with other first-line drugs. Its unique mechanism of action and favorable safety profile make it a valuable asset in the fight against TB.

Mechanism of Action

Ethambutol exerts its antimycobacterial effects by disrupting the synthesis of arabinogalactan, an essential component of the mycobacterial cell wall. By inhibiting the enzyme arabinosyl transferase, ethambutol interferes with the incorporation of arabinose into the cell wall, leading to structural abnormalities and impaired cell growth in Mycobacterium tuberculosis. This mode of action makes ethambutol particularly effective against actively replicating TB bacteria.

Medical Uses

1. **Treatment of Tuberculosis**: Ethambutol is a first-line anti-tubercular drug used in the treatment of both drug-susceptible and drug-resistant TB. It is often included in combination regimens with other first-line medications,

such as isoniazid, rifampicin, and pyrazinamide, to maximize efficacy and prevent the development of drug resistance.

2. **Prevention of Tuberculous Meningitis**: Ethambutol may also be used as part of prophylactic treatment regimens to prevent the development of tuberculous meningitis, a severe form of TB that affects the membranes surrounding the brain and spinal cord. When administered alongside other TB medications, ethambutol helps reduce the risk of TB dissemination to the central nervous system.

Dosage and Administration

Ethambutol is typically administered orally in the form of tablets or syrup. The dosage and duration of treatment vary depending on factors such as the patient's weight, age, and the severity of the TB infection. In standard TB treatment regimens, ethambutol is usually taken once daily, often for a duration of six to nine months. Dosage adjustments may be necessary in patients with renal impairment to prevent drug accumulation and toxicity.

Side Effects

While ethambutol is generally well-tolerated, it may cause side effects in some individuals. Common side effects may include:

- Visual disturbances (blurred vision, color vision changes)
- Gastrointestinal upset (nausea, vomiting, abdominal pain)
- Headache
- Rash
- Peripheral neuropathy (numbness, tingling, or

weakness in the extremities)

Of particular concern are visual disturbances, which can occur at higher doses or with prolonged treatment. Patients taking ethambutol should undergo regular ophthalmic evaluations to monitor for any changes in vision, and treatment should be discontinued if visual impairment occurs.

Para-Aminosalicylic Acid (PAS) :-

Para-aminosalicylic acid (PAS), also known as PAS or PASA, is a medication that has played a significant role in the treatment of tuberculosis (TB), particularly in cases of drug-resistant TB. This compound, first synthesized in the 1940s, represents a milestone in the history of TB therapy and continues to be an important component of anti-TB regimens, especially in regions where drug resistance is prevalent.

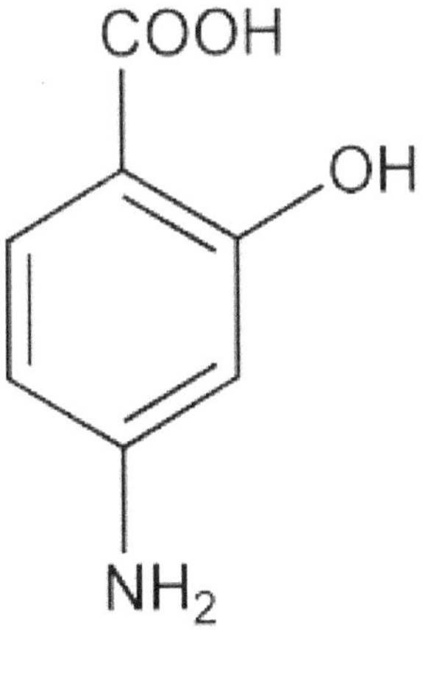

Mechanism of Action

PAS exerts its antimycobacterial effects by inhibiting the synthesis of folic acid, a crucial nutrient required for bacterial growth and replication. By interfering with the activity of dihydropteroate synthase, an enzyme involved in folic acid biosynthesis, PAS disrupts the metabolic pathways essential for the survival of Mycobacterium tuberculosis. This mechanism of action makes PAS particularly effective against actively dividing TB bacteria.

Medical Uses

1. **Treatment of Drug-Resistant Tuberculosis**: PAS is primarily used in the treatment of drug-resistant TB, including multidrug-resistant TB (MDR-TB) and extensively drug-resistant TB (XDR-TB). As a second-line anti-TB drug, PAS is often included in combination regimens with other second-line medications, such as fluoroquinolones, injectable agents, and other oral drugs, to enhance treatment efficacy and prevent the development of further drug resistance.

2. **Adjunctive Therapy for Drug-Susceptible Tuberculosis**: In some cases of drug-susceptible TB, PAS may be used as an adjunctive therapy when first-line medications are contraindicated or ineffective. It may be included in treatment regimens for patients with comorbidities, drug allergies, or intolerance to standard anti-TB drugs.

Dosage and Administration

PAS is typically administered orally in the form of tablets or granules. The dosage and duration of treatment vary depending on factors such as the patient's weight, age, and the severity of the TB infection. PAS is often prescribed in combination with other second-line anti-TB drugs, and treatment regimens may be tailored based on drug susceptibility testing and individual patient factors.

Side Effects

While PAS is generally well-tolerated, it may cause side effects in some individuals. Common side effects may include:

- Gastrointestinal disturbances (nausea, vomiting, abdominal pain)
- Loss of appetite
- Rash
- Hypersensitivity reactions

Rare but serious side effects may include hepatotoxicity (liver damage), hematologic abnormalities, and peripheral neuropathy. Patients should be monitored closely for signs of adverse reactions while taking PAS, and healthcare providers should be notified if any concerning symptoms develop

Anti-tubercular Antibiotics :- Tuberculosis (TB) remains a significant global health challenge, with millions of new cases and deaths reported each year. One of the most effective strategies for combating TB is the use of anti-tubercular antibiotics, medications specifically designed to target and eradicate Mycobacterium tuberculosis, the bacterium responsible for TB. These antibiotics play a crucial role in both the treatment and prevention of TB, helping to reduce morbidity, mortality, and transmission of the disease.

Overview of Anti-tubercular Antibiotics

Anti-tubercular antibiotics are a diverse group of medications that target various aspects of Mycobacterium tuberculosis biology, including cell wall synthesis, protein synthesis, and nucleic acid metabolism. These antibiotics are classified based on their mechanism of action and include first-line drugs, second-line drugs, and newer agents developed to combat drug-resistant TB strains.

First-Line Anti-tubercular Antibiotics

1. **Isoniazid (INH):** Isoniazid inhibits the synthesis of mycolic acids, essential components of the mycobacterial cell wall, by targeting the enzyme enoyl-ACP reductase (InhA). It is a cornerstone of TB treatment and is highly effective against actively dividing and dormant TB bacteria.
2. **Rifampicin (RIF):** Rifampicin inhibits bacterial RNA synthesis by binding to the bacterial DNA-dependent RNA polymerase. It is bactericidal against Mycobacterium tuberculosis and is used in combination with other first-line drugs for TB treatment.
3. **Pyrazinamide (PZA):** Pyrazinamide is particularly active against TB bacteria residing in acidic environments, such as within macrophages. Its mechanism of action involves disrupting mycobacterial cell membrane function and metabolism.
4. **Ethambutol (EMB):** Ethambutol disrupts mycobacterial cell wall synthesis by inhibiting the formation of arabinogalactan, a critical component of the cell envelope. It is often used in combination with other first-line drugs to prevent the emergence of drug resistance.

Second-Line Anti-tubercular Antibiotics

In cases of drug-resistant TB, second-line antibiotics are used as alternatives to first-line drugs. These antibiotics include:

- Fluoroquinolones (e.g., levofloxacin, moxifloxacin)
- Injectable agents (e.g., kanamycin, amikacin, capreomycin)
- Para-aminosalicylic acid (PAS)
- Cycloserine
- Linezolid
- Bedaquiline
- Delamanid

Newer Agents

Recent years have seen the development of newer anti-tubercular antibiotics, including:

- Bedaquiline: A first-in-class diarylquinoline antibiotic that targets mycobacterial ATP synthase, approved for the treatment of MDR-TB.
- Delamanid: A nitroimidazole derivative that inhibits mycolic acid synthesis, approved for the treatment of MDR-TB.
- Pretomanid: A nitroimidazole derivative with potent bactericidal activity against TB bacteria, used in combination regimens for drug-resistant TB.

Introduction to Drug Design
Overview

Drug design, also known as rational drug design, is the process of discovering and developing new medications based on the knowledge of a biological target. The goal is to design drugs that have a high affinity for their target, exhibit favorable pharmacokinetic properties, and are safe and effective for therapeutic use.

Key Concepts in Drug Design

1. **Target Identification and Validation**:

   - **Biological Target**: Typically a protein, enzyme, or nucleic acid involved in a disease pathway.
   - **Identification**: Using genomics, proteomics, and bioinformatics to identify potential targets.
   - **Validation**: Confirming the target's role in the disease through experimental techniques such as gene knockout, RNA interference, or use of small molecule inhibitors.

2. **Lead Compound Identification**:

   - **High-Throughput Screening (HTS)**: Testing thousands of compounds for activity against the target.
   - **Virtual Screening**: Using computer simulations to identify potential hits from large libraries of compounds.
   - **Fragment-Based Screening**: Screening small molecular fragments which bind to the target and can be chemically linked to form potent inhibitors.

3. **Lead Optimization**:

   - **Structure-Activity Relationship (SAR)**: Understanding the relationship between a drug's chemical structure and its biological activity.
   - **Medicinal Chemistry**: Modifying the chemical structure of lead compounds to improve potency, selectivity, and pharmacokinetic properties.

- **Computational Chemistry**: Using molecular modeling, docking studies, and simulations to predict the effects of structural changes.

4. **Pharmacokinetics and Pharmacodynamics (PK/PD):**

- **Absorption, Distribution, Metabolism, and Excretion (ADME)**: Studying how the drug is absorbed, distributed, metabolized, and excreted in the body.
- **Bioavailability**: The proportion of the drug that enters the circulation and reaches the target site.
- **Toxicology**: Assessing the potential toxic effects of the drug on the body.

5. **Clinical Development:**

- **Preclinical Testing**: In vitro and in vivo studies to evaluate the drug's safety and efficacy.
- **Clinical Trials**: Conducted in phases (Phase I, II, III, and IV) to further assess the drug's safety, efficacy, dosage, and side effects in humans.
- **Regulatory Approval**: Submitting data to regulatory bodies (e.g., FDA, EMA) for approval to market the drug.

Modern Approaches in Drug Design

1. **Computational Drug Design:**

- **Molecular Docking**: Predicting how small molecules, such as drugs, bind to a receptor.
- **Molecular Dynamics**: Simulating the physical

movements of atoms and molecules.

- **Quantitative Structure-Activity Relationship (QSAR)**: Developing models to predict the activity of new compounds based on the chemical structure of known compounds.

2. **Biologics and Biotechnology**:

- **Monoclonal Antibodies**: Engineered antibodies designed to bind specifically to target proteins.
- **Gene Therapy**: Delivering genetic material into cells to treat diseases by compensating for defective genes.
- **CRISPR/Cas9**: A gene-editing technology that allows for precise modifications to DNA.

3. **Artificial Intelligence (AI) and Machine Learning**:

- **AI Algorithms**: Analyzing large datasets to identify patterns and predict drug interactions and effects.
- **Machine Learning Models**: Optimizing the drug discovery process by predicting the efficacy and toxicity of compounds.

Approaches Used in Drug Design

Drug design involves various approaches, each tailored to different stages of the drug development process and aimed at improving the efficacy, selectivity, and safety of new therapeutic agents. Here are some of the primary approaches used in drug design:

1. High-Throughput Screening (HTS)

- **Description**: HTS is a method used to quickly assess

the biological activity of a large number of compounds. Automated systems test thousands to millions of compounds against biological targets in a rapid and efficient manner.

- **Applications**: Identifying lead compounds with desired biological activity from vast chemical libraries.

2. Structure-Based Drug Design (SBDD)

- **Description**: This approach uses the three-dimensional structure of a biological target, obtained through techniques like X-ray crystallography or NMR spectroscopy, to design molecules that fit precisely into the target's active site.
- **Applications**: Designing inhibitors that bind specifically to the active site of enzymes or receptors.

3. Ligand-Based Drug Design (LBDD)

- **Description**: LBDD relies on knowledge of molecules that bind to the target. It uses this information to design new compounds with similar or improved activity. Techniques include pharmacophore modeling and Quantitative Structure-Activity Relationship (QSAR) analysis.
- **Applications**: Creating new drug candidates based on the properties of known active compounds.

4. Fragment-Based Drug Design (FBDD)

- **Description**: FBDD involves screening small chemical fragments that bind to the target. These fragments are then optimized and combined to create potent lead compounds.

- **Applications**: Efficiently discovering starting points for drug development, especially for targets that are challenging for traditional HTS.

5. Computational Drug Design

- **Molecular Docking**: Predicts how small molecules fit into the binding site of a target protein, ranking them based on their binding affinity.
- **Molecular Dynamics (MD)**: Simulates the behavior of molecules over time, providing insights into the stability and conformational changes of drug-target complexes.
- **Virtual Screening**: Uses computational techniques to screen large libraries of compounds for potential biological activity.
- **QSAR Modeling**: Develops statistical models correlating chemical structure with biological activity, used to predict the activity of new compounds.

6. De Novo Drug Design

- **Description**: Involves designing new drug molecules from scratch based on the structure of the biological target. Algorithms generate novel compounds that are then tested for activity.
- **Applications**: Creating innovative compounds not found in existing libraries, potentially leading to novel therapeutic agents.

7. Biologics and Biotechnology

- **Monoclonal Antibodies**: Engineered antibodies that

specifically target proteins associated with diseases, used extensively in cancer and autoimmune diseases.

- **Peptide-Based Drugs**: Short chains of amino acids designed to mimic natural peptides with therapeutic effects.
- **Gene Therapy**: Introducing genetic material into cells to treat genetic disorders by correcting defective genes.

8. Artificial Intelligence (AI) and Machine Learning

- **AI Algorithms**: Analyze large datasets to identify potential drug candidates, predict biological activity, and optimize drug properties.
- **Machine Learning Models**: Improve the prediction of drug efficacy and toxicity, accelerating the drug discovery process.
- **Deep Learning**: Identifies patterns in complex biological data, aiding in the discovery of new drug-target interactions.

9. Pharmacokinetics and Pharmacodynamics (PK/PD) Modeling

- **Description**: Integrates data on how a drug is absorbed, distributed, metabolized, and excreted (ADME) and its pharmacological effects to optimize dosing regimens and predict therapeutic outcomes.
- **Applications**: Ensuring optimal drug concentration at the target site while minimizing side effects.

10. Chemical Biology Approaches

- **Chemical Probes**: Small molecules designed to interact

with a specific biological target, used to study biological processes and validate drug targets.

- **Activity-Based Protein Profiling (ABPP)**: Identifies active enzymes in complex biological samples, providing insights into enzyme function and drug interactions.

Quantitative Structure-Activity Relationship (QSAR) is a method used in drug design to predict the biological activity of compounds based on their chemical structure. QSAR models correlate physicochemical properties of molecules with their biological effects. Here are some key physicochemical parameters commonly used in QSAR:

1. Hydrophobicity (Lipophilicity)

- **Log P (Partition Coefficient)**: A measure of a compound's distribution between a hydrophobic (octanol) and hydrophilic (water) phase. It indicates the molecule's ability to cross cell membranes.
- **Log D**: The distribution coefficient that considers ionization at a specific pH. It is especially relevant for compounds that can be ionized under physiological conditions.

2. Electronic Properties

- **Hammett Substituent Constants (σ)**: Parameters that describe the electron-withdrawing or electron-donating effects of substituents relative to hydrogen.
- **Taft Steric Parameters (ES)**: Reflects the steric and electronic effects of substituents on reaction rates and equilibria.

- **Molecular Orbital Energy Levels (HOMO and LUMO)**: Highest Occupied Molecular Orbital (HOMO) and Lowest Unoccupied Molecular Orbital (LUMO) energies indicate the electron-donating and electron-accepting ability of molecules.

3. Steric Factors

- **Molar Refractivity (MR)**: A measure of the volume occupied by an atom or group of atoms, adjusted for polarizability.
- **Verloop Steric Parameters**: Quantitative measures of the spatial arrangement of substituents.
- **Steric Hindrance**: The physical obstruction encountered by a molecule due to the size and spatial orientation of its atoms or groups.

4. Topological Descriptors

- **Connectivity Indices (χ)**: Quantitative descriptions of a molecule's topology (branching patterns).
- **Wiener Index (W)**: Sum of the shortest paths between all pairs of vertices in a molecular graph.
- **Zagreb Indices**: Sum of the squares of the degrees of the vertices in a molecular graph.

5. Molecular Shape Descriptors

- **Kier and Hall Molecular Connectivity Indices**: Describe the molecular shape and branching.
- **Shape Index**: Quantifies the three-dimensional shape of a molecule, reflecting its geometry.

- **Eccentric Connectivity Index (ECI)**: Combines information on the connectivity and distance between atoms in a molecule.

6. Quantum Chemical Descriptors

- **Molecular Electrostatic Potential (MEP)**: Describes the charge distribution within a molecule.
- **Dipole Moment**: Measures the polarity of a molecule.
- **Polarizability**: Indicates how easily the electron cloud of a molecule can be distorted.

7. Thermodynamic Properties

- **Heat of Formation**: The change in enthalpy when a compound is formed from its elements.
- **Gibbs Free Energy**: The thermodynamic potential used to predict the direction of chemical reactions.
- **Entropy**: A measure of disorder or randomness in a system.

8. Miscellaneous Descriptors

- **Hydrogen Bond Donor/Acceptor Counts**: Number of hydrogen bond donors (NH, OH groups) and acceptors (O, N atoms) in a molecule.
- **Rotatable Bonds**: Number of single non-ring bonds that can rotate, affecting the molecule's flexibility.
- **Molecular Weight**: Total mass of a molecule, affecting its pharmacokinetic properties.

Application in QSAR

In QSAR modeling, these physicochemical parameters are used as input variables to build mathematical models correlating chemical structure with biological activity. The process typically involves:

1. **Data Collection**: Gathering experimental data on the biological activity of a series of compounds.
2. **Descriptor Calculation**: Computing the physicochemical parameters for each compound.
3. **Model Building**: Using statistical or machine learning techniques to develop a model that relates descriptors to biological activity.
4. **Validation**: Testing the model with independent datasets to ensure its predictive power.

Physicochemical Parameters and Hansch Analysis in QSAR

    1. Partition Coefficient (Log P)

- **Definition**: The partition coefficient, often expressed as Log P, is a measure of a compound's hydrophobicity. It represents the ratio of concentrations of a substance between two immiscible solvents (usually octanol and water) at equilibrium.
- **Formula**:

Log   P=log ([compound]??????[compound]?????)Log P=log([compound]$water$[compound]$octanol$)

- **Importance**: Log P is critical in predicting the absorption, distribution, metabolism, excretion (ADME), and toxicity of a compound. High Log P values generally indicate high lipophilicity, which can enhance cell membrane permeability but may also increase toxicity and decrease solubility in aqueous environments.

2. Hammett's Electronic Parameter (σ)

- **Definition**: Hammett's electronic parameter (σ) quantifies the electron-donating or electron-withdrawing effects of substituents relative to hydrogen in a benzene ring.
- **Calculation**: Determined by the substituent's influence on the dissociation constant (Ka) of benzoic acid derivatives.

$$?=\log (??,\text{substituted}??,\text{unsubstituted})\sigma=\log(Ka,\text{unsubstituted } Ka,\text{substituted})$$

- **Values**:

    - Positive σ values: Electron-withdrawing groups (e.g., nitro, cyano).
    - Negative σ values: Electron-donating groups (e.g., alkyl, methoxy).

- **Importance**: Used to predict the reactivity of compounds in various chemical reactions and the stability of intermediates.

3. Taft's Steric Parameter (Es)

- **Definition**: Taft's steric parameter (Es) measures the steric effects of substituents, representing the influence of the size and bulkiness of substituents on reaction rates and equilibria.

- **Calculation**: Derived from the rate constants of ester hydrolysis reactions, where steric effects are isolated from electronic effects.

$$??=\log\,(?unsubstituted?substituted)Es$$
$$=\log(ksubstitutedkunsubstituted)$$

- **Importance**: Important in understanding how the size and spatial arrangement of substituents affect the binding of molecules to their biological targets, influencing both potency and selectivity.

4. Hansch Analysis

- **Definition**: Hansch analysis is a QSAR method that correlates biological activity of compounds with their physicochemical properties, such as hydrophobicity (Log P), electronic parameters (σ), and steric factors (Es).
- **Process**:

  1. **Data Collection**: Gather biological activity data (e.g., IC50, EC50) for a series of compounds.
  2. **Descriptor Calculation**: Calculate relevant physicochemical parameters for each compound.
  3. **Model Development**: Use regression analysis to establish a mathematical relationship between the biological activity and the physicochemical descriptors.

Activity=?·Log P+?·?+?·??+?Activity=a·Log P+b·σ+c·Es+d where ?a, ?b, and ?c are coefficients determined by regression analysis, and ?d is a constant.

1. **Validation**: Validate the model with an independent dataset to ensure its predictive accuracy.

- **Importance**: Hansch analysis helps in understanding the contributions of different physicochemical properties to biological activity, guiding the design of new compounds with improved efficacy and reduced side effects.

Pharmacophore Modeling and Docking Techniques in Drug Design

Pharmacophore Modeling

Pharmacophore Definition: A pharmacophore is an abstract representation of the molecular features necessary for the optimal interactions with a specific biological target to trigger (or block) its biological response. These features include hydrogen bond acceptors, hydrogen bond donors, hydrophobic regions, aromatic rings, and charged groups.

Pharmacophore Modeling Process:

1. **Identification of Active Compounds**: Collect a set of compounds known to be active against the biological target.
2. **Feature Extraction**: Determine the common pharmacophoric features of these active compounds.
3. **Pharmacophore Hypothesis Generation**: Create a model (pharmacophore hypothesis) that maps out the essential features and their spatial arrangement.

4. **Validation**: Test the pharmacophore model against a dataset of active and inactive compounds to ensure its predictive accuracy.
5. **Screening**: Use the validated pharmacophore model to screen large chemical databases for new compounds that match the pharmacophoric features.

Applications:

- Identifying new potential drug candidates by virtual screening.
- Understanding the key interactions responsible for biological activity.
- Guiding the design and optimization of new compounds.

Docking Techniques

Molecular Docking Definition: Molecular docking is a computational technique used to predict the preferred orientation of a small molecule (ligand) when it binds to a protein (receptor) to form a stable complex. The goal is to predict the binding affinity and mode of interaction between the ligand and the target protein.

Docking Process:

1. **Preparation of Target and Ligand:**

   - **Target (Protein) Preparation**: Obtain the 3D structure of the target protein, typically from X-ray crystallography, NMR spectroscopy, or homology modeling.
   - **Ligand Preparation**: Prepare the 3D structures of the ligands, optimizing their geometry and ensuring they

are in the correct ionization and tautomeric states.

2. **Selection of Docking Algorithm**:

   - **Rigid Docking**: Both the ligand and the receptor are treated as rigid bodies.
   - **Flexible Docking**: The ligand is flexible, and sometimes the protein side chains in the binding site are also flexible.

3. **Scoring Function**: Apply a scoring function to estimate the binding affinity of the ligand for the protein. Scoring functions can be based on empirical data, force fields, or knowledge-based approaches.
4. **Docking Simulation**: Perform the docking simulation, generating multiple potential binding poses of the ligand in the active site of the protein.
5. **Analysis and Ranking**: Analyze and rank the docking results based on the scoring function. Select the top poses for further analysis.

Applications:

- **Lead Identification and Optimization**: Identifying new lead compounds and optimizing their binding affinity and specificity.
- **Mechanistic Studies**: Understanding the binding interactions and mechanisms of action of bioactive compounds.
- **Virtual Screening**: Screening large compound libraries to identify potential drug candidates that bind to the target protein.

Comparison of **Pharmacophore Modeling and Docking**:

- **Pharmacophore Modeling**: Focuses on identifying the key features required for biological activity and uses these features to screen for new compounds.
- **Docking Techniques**: Simulate the actual binding process of a ligand to its target protein, providing detailed information about the binding mode and affinity.

Integration of Both Techniques: Combining pharmacophore modeling and docking can enhance drug discovery efforts. Pharmacophore models can be used to pre-screen large libraries to identify potential hits, which can then be further refined and validated using docking studies to predict their binding modes and affinities.

Combinatorial Chemistry

Overview

Combinatorial chemistry is a method used in chemical synthesis to create large libraries of compounds by combining sets of building blocks in various ways. This approach significantly accelerates the discovery of new compounds with potential therapeutic value, as it allows for the simultaneous synthesis and screening of many molecules.

Key Concepts

1. **Chemical Libraries:**

   - **Definition**: Collections of diverse chemical compounds synthesized using combinatorial chemistry techniques.

- **Purpose**: To provide a broad array of molecules for screening against biological targets to identify hits (compounds with desirable biological activity).

2. **Building Blocks:**

- **Definition**: Basic chemical units used to construct more complex molecules.
- **Types**: Can include amino acids, nucleotides, or other organic molecules depending on the desired chemical diversity.

3. **Solid-Phase Synthesis:**

- **Definition**: A technique where reactants are bound to a solid support (like resin beads) and chemical reactions are carried out on this support.
- **Benefits**: Simplifies purification steps since unreacted reagents and by-products can be washed away, leaving the desired product attached to the solid support.

4. **Split and Pool Synthesis:**

- **Process:**

  1. **Split**: Divide the solid support into several portions.
  2. **React**: React each portion with different building blocks.
  3. **Pool**: Combine all portions together.
  4. **Repeat**: Repeat the process to add additional layers of diversity.

- **Outcome**: Creates a highly diverse library of compounds through iterative cycles of splitting, reacting, and pooling.

5. **Parallel Synthesis**:

   - **Definition**: Synthesizing compounds in parallel reactions, each in separate vessels, to create individual compounds rather than mixtures.
   - **Application**: Used when the purity of each compound is crucial for subsequent biological testing.

6. **Automated Synthesis**:

   - **Definition**: Utilizing robotics and automated systems to conduct chemical reactions, increasing efficiency and reproducibility.
   - **Benefits**: Allows for high-throughput synthesis and reduces manual labor and errors.

   Applications in Drug Discovery

1. **Lead Generation and Optimization**:

   - **Initial Screening**: Large libraries are screened against biological targets to identify lead compounds (hits).
   - **Optimization**: Hits are further modified to improve their potency, selectivity, and pharmacokinetic properties.

2. **SAR (Structure-Activity Relationship) Studies**:

- **Purpose**: To understand how variations in chemical structure affect biological activity.
- **Process**: Systematic modification of lead compounds to identify key functional groups responsible for activity.

3. **Development of Novel Therapeutics**:

- **Example**: Identification of new drug candidates for diseases with unmet medical needs by screening combinatorial libraries against disease-related targets.

Advantages

- **High Diversity**: Generates a vast number of structurally diverse compounds, increasing the chances of finding active molecules.
- **Efficiency**: Rapidly produces and screens large libraries, accelerating the drug discovery process.
- **Flexibility**: Adaptable to different types of chemical reactions and building blocks, enabling the exploration of various chemical spaces.

Challenges

- **Complexity of Mixtures**: Split and pool synthesis can create complex mixtures that are challenging to analyze and purify.
- **Resource Intensive**: Requires significant investment in automation and high-throughput screening technologies.
- **Data Management**: Handling and analyzing large

datasets generated from combinatorial libraries can be demanding.

Examples of Successful Applications

1. **Peptide Libraries**: Used to identify peptide-based drugs, inhibitors, or modulators of protein-protein interactions.
2. **Small Molecule Libraries**: Screening for enzyme inhibitors, receptor ligands, or other small molecule therapeutics.